The World's Best Sales Tips

"All things being equal, people will buy from a friend.
All things being not so equal, people will still buy from a friend."

Mark H. McCormack

For My Best Friends,

Kathy,

Fionnuala and Daniel

The World's Best Sales Tips

How to go from Zero to Hero

Ciaran McGuigan

early
coaching and
communication

Copyright © CJ McGuigan 2005
The right of CJ McGuigan to be identified as the moral rights author of this work has been asserted by him in accordance with the Copyright Amendment (moral rights) Act 2000.

All rights reserved. No part of this book may be reproduced or transmitted in any form or by any means, electronic or mechanical, including photocopying, recording or by any information storage and retrieval system, without prior permission in writing from the publisher.

First published in 2005
Early Coach Publishing, Sydney, New South Wales, Australia
Phone: 61 2 9222 9112
Email: mail@earlycoach.com
URL: www.earlycoach.com

National Library of Australia Cataloguing – in – Publication data:

McGuigan, C.J.
The world's best sales tips
Bibliography.
ISBN 0 9757229 0 5

1. Sales personnel. 2. Selling. I. Early Coaching and Communication (Association). II. Title.

658.85

Cover design and illustrations by Joseph Hollywood
Edited by Katherine McGuigan
Printed in Australia by McPherson's Printing Pty Ltd

Introduction

How many times have you bought a book on selling, sifted through hundreds of pages only to find just one or two ideas that you can use straight away?

Well in this book you can't turn one page without finding a new idea or practical selling tip. It has been written for those sales people hungry for ideas, tips and techniques that they can use instantly. Open at any page and read any tip in five minutes or less. Use it like a 'drop in' resource, available any time day or night when you need it.

Each of the tips has an icon next to them for easy subject identification. Whether you sell retail, industrial, corporate, over the phone or in the home, there are over 160 tips and techniques here that will help you make more money and have a more successful sales career.

My hope is that you keep it with you – in your brief case, glove box or next to your phone and that in years to come it will be 'dog-eared' from over use and be covered in margin notes. Open a page now and continue your journey to becoming the world's best.

Contents

Qualifying Tips
Are you keeping the post office in business?........................... 20
Qualify quicker and make your sales bigger! 41
Have you got $50,000? 88
Just say NO! 102
A real and present opportunity 111
From zero to hero! 143
Why don't you ask? 167

Telephone Sales Tips
Have an opening statement which creates interest 1
Voice mail 6
Getting call backs from voice mail 12
Stop losing money on incoming calls! 12
One more call a day 14
No hang ups 47
Telephone 'PIPS' 52
Voicemail 58
I'm at the airport 67
How do I sound? 67
Sounds interesting 72
Can you hold? 88
Do you know how to flash? 100
Call me back – no, you call ME back 104
Snatching defeat from victory 139
In the mood 142

VII

CONTENTS

Inquiry - interest - action 165
Their name is a key 166

👁

Finding New Business Tips
Explode your opportunities 4
Love thy neighbor 18
Who do you know? 26
If it is scarce, it MUST be good 34
Do your homework 36
Ps - where's your V Card? 51
'Own' the building, street, suburb.. 53
Reading 'windows' 74
The power of testimonials 74
Leveraging your lists.. 75
List management 77
Air mail 79
B.I.Y.E.R.S 80
REFERRALS 85
How much would you pay for a bucket of sand? 96
Double marketshare anyone? 101
The 'R' word 116
Networking - notworking.. 120
Chimney referrals 127
Have you met?.. 134
Sales Letters 158
There's always a niche.. 171

☑

Negotiating and Closing Tips
Trial closes 5
Their 'flinch' costs you 10%... 8
Moments of influence 22

VIII

CONTENTS

Splitting the difference 24
Alternatives and assumptives 27
You are the product 35
It's time to wake up, shake up and SERVICE your prospects. 41
Negotiating is NOT selling 45
Showroom sales – show me the money! 59
Avoid equal sized concessions 62
Show me the value! 76
Bargain - I don't think so 82
Reciprocal concession – 'Trumped'............................. 89
How much is that puppy in the window? 95
Sell to me in the kitchen... 103
Kindy sales lessons 106
The last minute... 119
The magic moment... 123
Get a handle on the outcome 123
Is that the best you can do? 129
Soft shoe sales... 137
Stop Selling.. 162

Time and Self Management Tips

The most expensive coffee you will ever drink... 6
Helping yourself with self help!................................... 11
Does your budget go on holiday too?......................... 17
Time is NOT on your side... 29
The ten minute rule 39
Less thought more action 40
Time Questions 43
'Danger, danger, Will Robinson…'.............................. 43
If you haven't got the time to do it right – when will you find the time to do it over?.. 53
Train yourself!... 59
Would you like $86,400? 61

IX

CONTENTS

If you haven't got a plan - you're a tourist! 64
Reticular? 91
Lead, follow or get out of the way............................. 107
Working longer and harder 111
Procrastination 114
Are you a $400,000k sales professional?..................... 115
Sales Housework 118
Right NOW!.. 120
Optimism 124
Paperwork panic.. 130
Rhetoric to reality... 138
Plan weekly - act daily 141
Readers are leaders... 141
Crisp and Green Do - Nots 146
Images and memory.. 150
Checklists 155
Budget your activity 158
Prioritize your prospects.. 159
Review and renew 169
Morning people.…... 170

Presenting and Pitching Tips
Who is presenting, you or Bill Gates?.......................... 9
Body language in the palm of your hand 16
Cowboys, priests, judges and hippies......................... 21
We're not really good at….. 28
How to write a great elevator speech......................... 55
Give me back that proposal!....................................... 68
Scribbled proposals... 70
VIP Presenting 93
Proposal pointers 98
Demonstrate before you 'presentate'......................... 99
Let them try before they buy 105

Get on your front foot 106
Story selling 110
And introducing... 126
The 3 components of a presentation 149
A picture is worth a thousand words (and $$$) 150
Make intangible – tangible 157

Building Relationships Tips
Let me scratch your back.... 10
What being 'professional' really means 37
Treat different customers differently 48
Be consistent 54
Indifferent? who cares? 63
Look into my eyes… 66
Are you an expert of choice? 71
Decision acceleration management 83
Sometimes it pays to be inconsistent 108
Your staff are your customers 127
Referee 154
Support Staff? 160

Dealing With Objections Tips
I want to think about it 15
Discounting disasters 23
'Yes' lives in the land of NO 37
No thanks, we're happy with our current supplier 44
Feel, felt, found 46
Managing the 'Not interested' response 57
'RUST' never sleeps 70
Are you a packhorse? 78
Remember this? 84

XI

CONTENTS

No forever?.. 92
No thanks we're happy.. 112
More 'RUST'... 116
I want to think it over... 131
How much too much? 134
I can't see the value.. 137
Your (product) doesn't work in our business 151
We have too much business already!...................... 153
I can get it cheaper... 169

Questioning and Listening Tips
That's a disturbing question 17
Is there anything else? 22
If your business was a 25
Are you prepared?... 29
What do your customers tell you?............................. 47
So what? 51
Before I begin... 87
Kick in the 'Buts'.. 94
Embedded commands 97
What's the difference?... 122
The 'reverse' Columbo 147
Difficult questions... 152
Problem / Potential 156
Questioning 163
Why is that important?... 166

The World's Best Sales Tips

Have an opening statement which creates interest

Let's look at the prospective phone call from the client's point of view. It is Monday morning about 10.00 a.m. They are getting stuck into their to-do list, schedule of appointments and various projects. They have a busy schedule and like a lot of other decision makers in their company, their time is important. In fact it is their most critical finite resource, so they guard it jealously.

Now their PA is good at balancing their diary and keeping unsolicited calls from getting through although, occasionally, the odd one does make it. However, they can recognize a pitch in a nanosecond and can politely (sometimes not so) get rid of them. This is a typical environment that your prospecting call is going into. What do you say to make your chances of securing a sale or an appointment as high as possible?

Let's look at what the 'average' sales rep says:

> "Good morning, my name is John Doe from Superior Services, the reason I am calling you today is I just wanted to let you know…touch base…was wondering…was in the area…"

There is a science to creating great opening statements and this is THE most critical stage of the prospecting process. Fundamentally, you must sound pleasant and confident and quickly offer proof of how you helped someone just like them by reducing their PAIN (what they want less of) and increase their GAIN (what they want more of) all in less than 20 seconds! As a first step, write yourself a script and

✓ **Quick TIP**: Focus on the emotional – what does your prospect want?

review it, do you sound interesting? If not, dump it and try again.

Tape yourself and keep going until you get it right. What are the critical issues for their industry, market and business? Make sure you identify and offer proof of two things; how you can reduce what they want less of and how you can help them get more of what they want.

Below, is an opening statement that I have highlighted and broken down the five elements which make it work. I encourage you to take your own statements and break them down in this way:

> "Is that David DeCision?
> Hi David, my name is Peter Sells of World's Best Widgets.
>
> David, the reason I wanted to speak with you today is that my company and I have recently been working with several other major businesses in your industry; ABC and XYZ industries.
> We've been helping them not only cut (slash / halve / shrink etc) the amount of labour, administrative time and management required for most widget installations,
> but at the same time doubling the effective life and profitability of each component used in the process. I would love to come by some time and show you how we did that."

Element ONE: The Greeting / Introduction

This confirms you are speaking to the right person and also tells them who you are and where you are calling from:

> *"Is that David DeCision? (YES) Hi David, my name is Peter Sells of World's Best Widgets."*

Element TWO: Proof you have helped others like them

This builds a genuine reason for your call based on the good work you have done for others:

> *"David, the reason I wanted to speak with you today is that my company and I have recently been working with several other major businesses in your industry (use people and company names if possible) helping them not only"*

Element THREE: Reduce their PAIN

This focuses on what drives most decisions; what is it your prospects want less of and where are the areas of their business giving them most pain:

> *"cut (slash / halve / shrink etc) the amount of labour, administrative time and management required for most widget installations, but at the same time"*

Element FOUR: Increase their GAIN

This focuses on the other major driver in decision making: what is it they want more of:

> *"doubling the effective life and profitability of each component used in the process."*

Element FIVE: TRIAL CLOSE Appointment

This phrase invites them to agree to an appointment, or more likely respond to you with a question / objection:

> *"I would love to come by some time and show you how we did that."*

What next?

An objection or a question is the most likely initial response from your prospect. Stay focused on the reason why they should meet with you and keep the results you have achieved for others the key topic. For another look at this technique see page 72.

Explode your opportunities

When I use the term 'Explode Your Opportunities' I want you to do just that, not go out and use a couple of sticks of dynamite, but create a map to show your existing relationships with your existing customers and THEIR customers. Here's how to do it:

Identify a client who is delighted with your product or service. Now get hold of a whiteboard or a clean sheet of paper and put your client's name in the center of one page in a circle. Spend a couple of minutes and identify six businesses / individuals who also sell products and services to your client. I like to draw each one of them in a 'circle' centred around, and connected to, the key relationship. In this way you can 'drill down' into each subset to explore the relationships.

Make sure you ask your current client for permission to contact this network and that you have some illustration, demonstration or **proof** of how your service helped them through a challenge.

The key to using this is twofold. Even if you only have a small client base of six, by using this system, you immediately have at least **36 new businesses** to contact

THE WORLD'S BEST SALES TIPS

AND you will be in a position to leverage your existing relationship! As each new relationship develops you can continually expand this model and in a very short period of time 'Explode' your potential for business growth.

Trial closes

What is the difference between a trial close and an actual close? There is a lot of literature available on the 'Net' and in the local bookshop. The easiest and most useful definition I know is this; a trial close asks for an opinion, whereas an actual close asks for a decision.

Now, in my opinion, a lot of sales people make a fundamental mistake and believe that in order to be successful in sales they need to be hard closers. They equate this with asking for decisions and then push too early in the sales process. For the prospect the easiest answer is NO. Some of the best sales people I have ever worked with almost **NEVER** make the close themselves, they let the **CLIENT** close the deal.

They achieve this by using trial closes in the same way a chef uses seasoning, a lot sprinkled around. One of the best and most successful trial closing scripts is the following:

"...makes sense to me, what do you think?"

You can use this after running through the benefits of your product or service. Based on the answer from the prospect, you can move forward or go back and address their concern. Of course, after you deliver your trial close you need to use one of the best techniques of all: **SHUT UP** and wait for their response.

Voice mail

For most of us in sales, leaving messages on voice mail is a way of life. If you are trying to reach decision makers, (their time is valuable) you need to leave a message which gives them a **REASON** to call you back. A lot of the work that you put into creating a great opening statement *(see page 1)* can really help here. Here are a few tips for leaving an effective voicemail.

Make sure that you leave your phone number at the beginning and end of the message, you cannot be sure that your prospect will go back to the start to listen again to your pitch. Also, think of what you can say that will make them want to call you back as soon as they hear the message.

You have to make sure your tone is confident, well paced and has authority. The easiest way to do this is to start recording yourself. I have not met many executives who liked the way they sound, but that's the reality of how you sound to prospects. Having done that, you can begin to start changing and controlling your tone for the better.

One more thing, try this; if you are leaving a voice mail message, flip the phone over and speak into the mouthpiece as if it were a microphone in your hand, you will be surprised at how much better you will sound.

The most expensive coffee you will ever drink...

What is the first thing you do every day when you arrive at work? There are hundreds of thousands of sales teams and executives in the marketplace who have the sales talent, but there are considerably less who can match it with continuous prospecting activity!

I have seen many talented people fail because of a lack of activity, particularly account managers. This does not mean they are not busy, they are usually incredibly busy. Ask them. There is not enough time in the day, they work longer hours are stressed and generally have a sense of 'incompleteness' at the end of a day.

Does this sound familiar? What I discovered was on the days that I made some outbound proactive prospecting calls, I went home feeling a LOT better.

A proactive prospecting call is to someone you have never spoken to before. Don't kid yourself by calling your friendly clients, family, friends and sales colleagues. These will not make you competitively successful. You can make those calls later. On those days when I allowed admin, red tape and just 'doing stuff' to take over my diary, at the end of the day I was tired and stressed!

Put yourself in the shoes of just about any sales manager in the country. You are interviewing candidates for a new sales position in your company and when you ask them: Why should I hire you? The candidate says;

> "Because before I do anything else, every day I make at least ten new calls to clients I have never spoken to."

Now, I suspect that after they say this, they will be a lot closer to getting the position than the others in the hallway!

Here is the system I want to share with you. It's called: 10 x 10. Every day make 10 outgoing calls to new prospects before 10 am! This means that the FIRST thing you do is make those calls, before coffee, reading e-mails, chatting and catching up with colleagues. This is your JOB. It doesn't matter if you can't get through or get voice mail / rejected. Start on this process make it a habit and it will pay off.

Of course there will be meetings and appointments etc., which will force you to occasionally change this pattern, that's fine, just adapt your weekly diary to pick up the slack.

Their 'flinch' costs you 10%

☑ Most sales training environments train you how to negotiate with a potential buyer. Here is a key insight into a technique YOUR prospects have probably been TRAINED in. If you think that buyers don't receive training in this, don't kid yourself, in a lot of ways they measure their success by the effectiveness of their negotiations with you.

I am sure most of you will recognize this powerful and simple technique; The 'FLINCH'. Tradespeople are great at this. What is the first thing a plumber does when he looks under your sink or when a mechanic looks under your car bonnet? He shakes his head, there might be a 'tut tut', and then an audible intake of breath or a physical reaction (flinch) as if he had touched something red hot. Perhaps he even asks a question like: …who did this work? - were they a licensed …(plumber / mechanic etc)?

So what are they doing? By 'flinching', when they first see the job, they are influencing our expectations. What we previously thought would be a simple job, now may not be all that easy, and we haven't even begun to negotiate yet!

Your prospects may also have been trained to flinch when you mention a price or anything which gives them an opportunity to exact pressure. You need to recognize this and disarm it.

So how do you do that? It really is quite simple, don't react! Keep a straight face and ask them if they were trained to do it and praise them for a great flinch. Most of the time your prospect will capitulate and praise YOU for noticing. You can then progress with your sale!

Who is presenting, you or Bill Gates?

Whenever you are preparing for a presentation, don't let PowerPoint act as your coach. Your audience will thank you. Too many executives allow their ppt presentation to act as their leave behind document and their delivery script as well. But these are very different components and you NEED to treat each one differently.

Here's what you need to do the next time you are preparing for a presentation. Make sure your visual display is clear, clean and attractive. Your document should contain all the necessary detail that you have **not** presented, things such as appendices, research, links, etc., and make sure your delivery has been rehearsed. Concentrate on your body language, tone of voice and eye contact.

If you can get access to the room, stand in the spot where you will be presenting, feel the size of the room and rehearse your opening statements. Walk around and sit where a typical audience member will sit and ask a few questions. Can I see and hear the presenter from this position? Can I see the flipchart and are the colors and illustrations that I have used clearly visible?

Within this context the key to an effective presentation is your understanding of **THEIR** state of mind prior to the presentation and what you need to do to change that!

Let me scratch your back....

Robert Cialdini illustrates the power of reciprocity several times in his essential book, 'Influence'. It is the first of his six universal rules of persuasion. Roger Dawson describes sales as a persuasion contest and he is right. So what is reciprocity and how can you use it as a sales professional?

Have you ever attended a dinner party at a colleague's house and felt guilty several months later because you have still not invited them over to your place?

There is an implicit expectation when you are a guest of someone that you will repay the favor some day! This could be many months, even years later! Now this only works if the other person places a personal VALUE on what you have done for them.

Spend a few minutes now and make two lists; one of those things that are of low or no cost to you, the other of issues, concerns and challenges your prospect needs help with. The next stage is critical. I want you to offer to help them with one of their issues by providing something from your list. Do this without charging for it or creating the expectation of a trade. By providing something which they truly value, you will distinguish yourself and build a strong foundation for a profitable relationship.

Helping yourself with self help!

The number of sales people in the marketplace who have had little or no sales training constantly amazes me. There are those who had a day of training or listened to some tapes 3, 4 or 5 years ago and believe it is enough!

Are you still using the same methodology and database and systems you were last year or five years ago and still expecting to get better results? Don't be surprised when the results are pretty much like previous years / quarters / months?

Research conducted several years ago found that of those people who bought self improvement books, approximately 10% actually finish the book and only 10% of those who finish actually do something about their behavior as a result of the contents. If only one in one hundred people took action, why did the other 99 not?

I believe that most people think that buying the book and reading it is enough. It is not. The difference between ordinary and extraordinary is very small and it is the last step TAKING ACTION, that makes all the difference.

If you have a few 'How to...' books sitting around, take one of them, read it and re-read it, summarize the main points into a mind map and one at a time translate the techniques into ACTION. If you start doing this **you** are in the 1%.

Getting call backs from voice mail

Voice mail is a way of life in business, if you are to succeed you need to get better at generating replies. Here are a couple of short and simple techniques that work.

I'll be at your place: If your prospect has not returned your calls, here is a voice mail message that will get a response;

> "Mr Prospect, a major client of mine (mention name) is in the same (building, street, city) as you and I am meeting with them next Tuesday. Could we meet at your place after this, at 2.00pm on the 23rd? If I have not heard back from you I shall see you there, however if you can't make this time please call me back on 1234 5342."

I know how busy you are:

> "Mr Prospect, It's John Doe here from ABC supplies, I know how busy you are and I don't want to waste either of our time. If you would like to be taken off my contact list, please call 0404 1234 4325. If I don't hear from you I will try to reach you in a few days."

Stop losing money on incoming calls!

If you are a sales manager or you own your own business, the chances are that you are losing about twenty percent in potential sales. If only one in five calls are missed = **20% lost**! Think of the dollars, effort and advertising, direct mail shots, telemarketing campaigns, box drops and all the other strategies employed just to do one thing, make the phone ring! Missing out on this revenue is the same as closing your business for **TWO MONTHS**! Can you afford to do that?

People who are shopping around **don't call back** (even when they say so!) because the chances are that the next company they ring will offer them great service and their inquiry will be dealt with professionally and promptly. They won't NEED to call you.

So before you spend another dollar on marketing and promotions, before you spend another two hours writing copy for your newsletter, mailshot or phone script. Before you spend any money on training your sales team to prospect, present and negotiate, make sure that everyone (not just the sales team!) knows how to deal with an incoming call!

The key thing here is that throughout the company each person has to know that the person who answers the phone has the RESPONSIBILITY for the quality of the service for that call. For example;

"Good morning, 123 Services, John Doe speaking - how can I help you?"

No phone should ring more that three times without some one answering it. No one should be on hold for more than twenty seconds. Whoever takes the call should answer using your company's phone answering policy. If, after all this the required person is still not available, asking them to call back later will lose a sales opportunity.

The person taking the call should be in a position to say when (approximately) John Doe will be available. They

✓ **Quick TIP**: Always ask – is there anything else? When you think you have covered everything.

13

should get the contact's name and number, when they can be contacted and also ascertain if THEY can do anything NOW to help them.

This is really simple stuff but it makes a big difference. As you call different companies listen to the way they greet you and how that makes you feel. Here are four simple steps to increasing your business by managing incoming calls better:

- Create a phone answering policy
- Make it bold and simple and easy to remember
- Print and distribute them to every phone
- Be vigilant in the adoption of the policy

One more call a day

Seemingly small changes can occasionally generate big rewards. What would happen if at the end of each day, when you have planned your next day, turned the PC off, packed your bag and are just about to walk out the door- if you made one more prospecting call?

Well first of all you would make over **200 MORE** calls each year. You and I both know that this would result in increased business. So, today when you have your coat on and you are just about to run out the door, take 30 seconds and dial one more number. Consider your average client value. If you are in B2B (business to business) sales, if only 5% of those extra calls turn into clients (**10 new clients!**) that 30 seconds each day is time very well spent.

I want to think about it

When a prospect tells you they want to 'think about it' or 'think it over' it is easy for you to concede and agree to call them back in a week / month / whenever! But the reality is that the chances of you closing the business at the 'next' meeting have reduced substantially, if not totally.

It doesn't have to be like this. When a prospect tells you they want to think it over, it is actually a great opportunity to close the deal. Let me illustrate how to deal with this objection, which can cost you a fortune if not handled properly. Let's assume that I sell office machines, my prospect has just told me that he would like to think about it. My reply is:

> "John, are you saying that because you want to think about which model is best suited to your needs or are you saying that because you think the price is too high?"

Nine times from ten the prospect will say either; "yeah, the price is too high" or a variant of this such as; "it's a bit more than we budgeted for."

When they say this, reply:

> **"How much too high do you think it is?"**

Let's say that they say $1000. It could be any amount, it does not really matter, your reply should be:

> **"Other than price, is there anything else which would stop you from moving forward?"**

At this point most people will say NO. Now you are in a much more powerful position than when the original objection was given. In reality, the sale has taken place and it is now a negotiation, we can either add value or offer a better outcome based on their critical issues.

Body language in the palm of your hand

Body language has a huge impact on how effectively you communicate with and influence others face to face. Often when I work on 'body language' in a sales training program most people in the room initially think of the large arm gestures, eye contact and entire physiology. These are important, but there is one very powerful technique, which is seldom consciously noticed but when used properly can position the sales person with power and authority.

The position of the palm of your hand can change the whole context of your verbal and other nonverbal messages to your prospect. There are three main gestures; Palm up, Palm down and Palm closed and finger pointed. You can take any statement or question delivered in a face to face sales situation and if all other signals (tone of voice, eye contact etc) remain the same, the communication will probably be received differently depending on your hand position in relation to the timing of your question.

Try it with a colleague in your office. Ask them if they notice anything. Generally an open palm indicates a request, palm down communicates that you are in authority and palm closed and finger pointing can be seen as aggressive and an instruction or command. This almost imperceptible change in body language can completely change your meaning.

That's a disturbing question

There are many different types of questions available to the sales professional. One of my favorites is what I call asking a 'disturbing' question. I don't use it all the time, but when needed, it can transform a discussion into a sale! So how does it work? The fundamental basis for this question is to change the prospect's paradigm.

I want them to explore and consider all the options of an action either taking or not taking place, in particular when one of my product / service features addresses this need.

If, for instance, I sold refrigeration equipment to retailers and one of my product's features was a back to base automated failure phone notification system, a straightforward disturbing question could be;

> "What would happen to your frozen stock and revenues if your equipment failed in the middle of the night?"

Create a few questions of your own and trial them in your next sales call.

Does your budget go on holiday too?

Think about traditional holiday periods in your business. For example, have you already written off December and January as low sales months?

Do you know why your sales budgets are probably lower in one or both of these months than in others? Probably because they were based on the previous year's! The easy option is to accept that an average performance last year means the same this season. If your sales come about because of your skill and activity then you know this season can be whatever you want it to be! All you have to do is pick up the phone...

Love thy neighbor

A famous Harvard business school professor once asked his students what was the number one reason businesses do not succeed. Of course, as he expected, he received all types of responses; poor management, cash flow, faulty products, the economy, government, regulation and many more, but not the number one reason. The number one reason why ANY business fails is; **'a lack of Sales.'**

As a salesperson, this is your responsibility. The word sales may not be on your business card but you need to engineer your business model around this fact. You need to have specific behaviors, which enhance the sales process.

Sales come from two places; your existing customers and new customers. You can 'search' for new business opportunities in three different ways:

> **Geographically, Demographically & Psychographically**

The ideal prospect falls into all of these categories. They are in your geographic reach, for instance your building, suburb, city, they are close to or fit your typical customer profile (demographic) and also have a predisposition (psychographic) towards your product / service.

I always start sales campaigns geographically. In fact, I always start with the building I am in. I get focused; there is no way I want anyone in my building buying the same products or services I offer without talking to me first! Can you say the same thing about your building? When I first moved into my city address, I spoke to every single business owner in my building and told them just this;

"...we are neighbors; we should meet and get to know each other!"

Just using this strategy, you can generate thousands of dollars in NEW business! The next time you walk into your building STOP. Take out a pen and write down the names of all the companies in the foyer. Then make it a priority to get their contact details and make it YOUR building, your street and your block.

Are you keeping the post office in business?

Across your city and around the world right now there are thousands of sales executives stuffing information into envelopes and sending them to what *they* WANT to think of as Hot Prospects. It is one of the oldest and easiest ways for busy people to get rid of sales calls. This works because the sales executive thinks it's a lead and that all they have to do is get the info into the prospect's hands and BINGO they will be on the phone desperate to buy!

Maybe a week later you call the 'prospect' with the "did you get the information" line. 99% of the time their response will be; "oh I haven't got to it yet, can you call me back next week?" Many more calls / voice mails and wasted time later the prospect is too far in to admit that they STILL have not read it.

So what do they do? They tell you that after reading it they have made a decision NOT to use your product / service at this time, but call us again in a few months time. Average sales people then start offering discounts.

Generally speaking don't send out information unless you have qualified them well and the reason for the info is really justified. Pay close attention to the questions they are asking, and note how long you have been speaking to them. Sending information to someone you have been speaking to for 15 minutes is a lot better than a two-minute call.

If possible, arrange an appointment to present the information but most importantly ask them;

> "Mr Prospect, what sort of information would be most important to you in order to make an informed decision about this?"

If they don't know you are probably wasting your time and if they do, you can move forward with the sales process.

Cowboys, priests, judges and hippies

When working with executives on a major pitch or presentation and I need to minimize their nervousness and maximize their delivery and confidence, there is a simple technique that always works. You can use it, it may seem a little odd at first but your presentation performance will be so much better.

Often the greatest challenge in a corporate presentation environment is seeing the real person or the human side, behind the PowerPoint presentation. When preparing for your next presentation, try to find a room where you can rehearse in private. Run through the first five minutes or so as you normally would. Next, I want you to keep the same content but again go through the first five minutes or so but this time acting as a COWBOY.

For instance, pretend to be a John Wayne type of character. Change you voice tone, posture, emphasis etc. Then run through the same exercise as a Priest, then a Judge and then a Hippie. After 20 minutes of this, return to your 'old' self and I can guarantee that your performance will be substantially better. Don't take my word for it, try it out for yourself!

Is there anything else?

This one question has turned small sales into large deals, it has saved me time, worry and stress and is now a key component of my sales language and it should be part of yours. When I think I have covered everything I ask; "is there anything else I haven't covered?".

By asking this question I am ensuring that my prospect has had the opportunity to voice their concerns, thoughts or objections BEFORE we finish the sales call. Many times when you ask this question your prospects come back to you with something that you thought you had covered.

Moments of influence

Throughout this book *(pages 10, 123)*, I touch on the power of reciprocity in sales and how you can leverage this universal rule. Do you know what you should do when a prospect says 'thank you'. Cialdini calls this a moment of power, he is right and it lasts just seconds. There is a window of opportunity here where you have a chance to generate support from a prospect or you can just let it fly out the window.

Let's create an example. You know that a particular prospect of yours has been having trouble getting information on African Coffee beans. You are in the soft drink business but you suspect that one of your contacts has the information your prospect needs. A few phone calls and e-mails later you have the data and you send it over to your prospect with a short note mentioning that you hope this is the info they were looking for. What happens now?

Well, we are using the concept of reciprocity and indeed the prospect may be grateful but most people will DROP the ball when the prospect phones in to say thanks. MOST people will say something like, '...that's OK anyone would have done it....' or '...don't think anything of it, I had the information on my desk....' Most people will down play the effort they put in. Don't be most people!

There is a simple technique I want you to use whenever a prospect says 'Thank you' and that is;

> "That's ok, I know that you would do the same for me"

Just reading this you may be able to sense the difference in the two responses. Your reply can either make it a gift or a trade. This technique works everywhere. Try it the next time a work colleague is asking for a lot of favours continuously or you feel a friend is taking advantage of your generosity. You can use this only after they say thank you...

A word of warning, when they say thanks don't say 'oh yeah and you owe me!' that tends to generate the opposite reaction!

Discounting disasters

Do you know what sort of an impact discounting has on your sales performance? When I am training negotiation skills, most sales executives tell me that they don't consider a 10% discount to be all that much.

If a sales executive has a budget of $100, and the sticker price is $10.00, you don't have to be a genius to figure that they need ten sales at $10 to make budget. Now if the cost of goods is $7.00 then the overall profit budget is $30.00. If our hypothetical sales person has not been trained in negotiating, they may be suffering from terminal discounting and not know it.

It is a serious issue. If our salesperson is discounting on average only by 10% the impact is massive. The key here is understanding that our PROFIT budget has not changed. We still need to reach $30.00 but now we are only making $2.00 on each unit rather than $3.00. When you do the numbers, what you discover is that our sales person has to make 15 sales to reach the same profit. They need an increase of over 50% in successful sales!

When you discount it comes off your bottom line and probably trebles in impact, your costs don't change. All you have to do is work harder at finding new sales. If you have to work harder why not do it earlier rather than later and sell based on value rather than price?

Splitting the difference

☑ Often in a negotiation the parties will be at a point where they have got as far as they believe they can go. It can seem that the most logical thing to do is to 'split' the difference and agree on a price. As a professional sales person you do not want to be the person making this offer first, but you do want them to make it to you. It is hard not to make the first offer. You almost need to be walking out the door saying that it is a shame you can't do business together only because of ($$$ figure), if only we could find a way forward...

But isn't the price the same either way? Not really. Let me explain why. If your prospect makes the offer to split the difference you have the opportunity to 'split' the difference again. All you need to do is defer to a higher authority (ie. make a private phone call to your boss) to see if they will accept the offer. When you go back into the prospect's office you can 'flinch' *(see page 8)*, and tell them that their offer was rejected but your boss is willing to split the new difference. You will be surprised at the number of prospects who will move forward with this.

If your business was a ....

Here is a great questioning technique that you can use to really get into the mindset of your prospect. It uses the power of a metaphor to create a frame or gateway for you into their understanding. As a technique it should be used after some level of rapport has been established.

Here is an example of how it works; "John, if your business was a type of car, what type of car would it be?" They might reply by saying a Ford, Ferrari, or Mack Truck. You then have an opportunity to ask; Why did you choose that one?

This is where the value of this technique comes in, they start describing and you start LISTENING. The feedback you will get will give you invaluable insight into their needs and a solid platform to sell from.

Who do you know?

Earlier I wrote about the value of asking; "is there anything else?" Now I want to expand on that and focus on referral prospecting and a few simple steps to doing this correctly.

All the best sales professionals KNOW that referrals are the best form of leads. It is not a hard or difficult process yet most sales people don't ask. For some there is a sense that the client has just made a commitment to buy from you and you should take the order and run out of their office ASAP! But resist the temptation.

The conversion rates between referred leads and a successful sale is substantially higher than a cold prospect. Why is this? When you contact a referral for the first time you have 'deferred trust'. What I mean is you and the prospect have no relationship as yet, but because your client and prospect do, the prospect is prepared to give you some 'latitude'.

There is a simple process for asking for referrals:

Look after the client's order BEFORE you make a request

You must have completed the sale. This can be a challenge, particularly if the client volunteers referrals unprompted. I suggest you make a note and tell your prospect that you would like to come back to that in a moment, followed by an open question, which will get your sales process back on track!

Create a 'Bridge' to the request

When the client has made a commitment and you are satisfied with your outcome, use a 'bridging' technique to move towards your request. A 'bridge' is just a phrase or statement that allows you to introduce a new question, topic or focus. Something like;

> "...John, just one more thing..."
>
> "...Peter, while you are at your desk...."
>
> "...Jane, before I go...."

Ask for the referral and emphasize the benefits

> "...John, thank you for your order, just one more thing, who do you know who has the same needs for (highlight the benefits as your client sees them) that I would also be able to help?

The key thing here is that you are asking, "Who do you know?" rather than "DO you know?" Your chances are substantially higher with the first example because 'Do you know' is a closed question and it is too easy to answer with a NO.

Alternatives and assumptives

☑ The 'Assumptive' close is probably the #1 closing technique on the planet. I would be amazed if most of you and your colleagues are not aware of and are using it on a regular basis. As the name implies, the technique 'assumes' the sale decision has been made and in this way you are not asking for approval regarding a major purchase decision but the 'OK' on a smaller more administrative detail.

Personally I think this works best when you also present a couple of alternatives, then we have an 'alternative assumptive' close. Delivered as a closed question to your prospect it can take you straight to the final sale. Let's look at an example.

> "John, is your preference for the goods to be delivered in the morning or in the afternoon?"
>
> "So, what would work best for you, the blue or pink curtains?"
>
> "Would you like your logo to appear at the top or at the bottom of your ad?"

An essential requirement of this technique is that you **SHUT UP** after you deliver the question. Not a sound. No 'mms' or 'ahhs'. It can take a while to get used to doing this but the next person who makes a sound 'owns it'.

We're not really good at…..

How can presenting your weakest point FIRST be a good thing? It is not all that complicated really. When you are presenting to a 'cold' prospect (by cold I mean some one who has no relationship with you) they don't trust you. They have no reason to. In fact they probably have every reason to treat what you say with some caution. After all you are a sales person, it says so on your business card!

I want you to consider presenting your weakest point first in this type of scenario because it makes your next point your strongest. You will appear so much more credible, believable and trustworthy. You create a sense of honesty and, don't kid yourself, your competition is probably going to highlight your weak points. So disarm them with a pre-emptive strike and gain some valuable trust points at the same time.

Time is NOT on your side

Many teams and executives will spend a LOT of time planning budgets, targets and strategies. That's all valuable stuff, however it does not come first. Your first activity has to be managing your sales time effectively. Most plans end up in a plastic binder and are looked at once a year.

I suggest that before you plan anything you devote at least 20% of your total diary time to prospecting activity, that is TALKING to prospects. Measure your $$$ performance monthly but manage your weekly budget by ACTIVITY not dollars.

Manage your goals quarterly and plan each week's activity on a Sunday evening. Do not plan on a day by day basis. If you work in a large office allow 30 - 40% of your total time for unplanned interruptions.

Are you prepared?

This is probably one of the most valuable prospect interview and questioning techniques I have ever used. It is a development of a technique originally used by Allan Pease in his book; 'Questions are the Answers'. Often, with a lot of techniques and processes there are a large number of things you need to remember. The beauty of this is that it is EASY to recall AND use when you need it.

One of the most important things to remember when you are meeting a prospect for the first time is that they are buying YOU before they think of your product or service. It is not good enough to ask good questions, they have to feel that you understand their point of view both emotionally and rationally.

Another key aspect worth remembering from your prospect's point of view is that if you say something, it is debatable whether they think it is true or not. Even if they say they agree with you. However, if THEY say something then it HAS to be true. All you need to get them to do is to say things that can help you make a successful sale.

If you use this tip you will enjoy more business, happier customers and a competitive advantage. At the end of the process your prospect will have TOLD YOU what is important to them emotionally and rationally and why. The next step is fairly simple, you can then tie in your product or service with their stated fears and goals.

What you have to do is **PREPARE** your questions. PREPARE is an acronym for the following questioning technique:

P:	Priority?
R:	Rational Question
E:	Emotional Question
P:	Pro – towards the priority
A:	Anti – away from the priority
R:	Rational Question
E:	Emotional Question

Let's take a look at how this works. Here is a great question to ask your prospect;

> "John, there are many challenges for businesses in today's market...what do you see as the major critical issues for your success in the next year or so (or other time period)?"

While they are giving you the 5 - 6 items, take notes and write them down in bold, clear lettering. If they only give you one or two issues, ask for more. When you have the list, thank them and show them the page and ask the first question in the PREPARE model; The question you need to ask is;

"Which one out of all of these is your #1 PRIORITY?"

Once they answer, you can then ask your first Rational Question:

"Why did you choose that?"

This question is asking them to explain how they have prioritized their critical issues. The information you will receive will usually be unemotional, logical and rational based on facts and evidence, data, sales figures, market share, etc.

Our next question is Emotional and is designed to generate a personal answer, in other words, information about their FEELINGS regarding this issue:

"Why is that important to you?"

The second and third questions you asked were PRO, meaning towards, and were focused on moving you towards an understanding of their outcomes. The next two questions are ANTI (away) and are designed to generate responses that get your prospect to focus on the implications for NOT achieving outcomes.

The next (fourth) question is rational, and is the first question designed to get our prospect thinking in a new way:

"What are the consequences of this NOT happening?"

Again at this stage they will give you fairly logical answers based on evidence and history. As you are taking notes and keeping eye contact and maintaining rapport (remember at no stage do you want your sales questions to feel like an interrogation) you are ready to ask your final question in the model.

Our final (fifth) question is an Emotional question and focuses on their personal concerns regarding the consequences:

"Why would that worry you?"

If you have followed this model and have maintained rapport, you will now be in a much more powerful position to begin your sales proposal.

Below I have applied the model in a 'scripted' scenario to illustrate how easy this is to remember, use and sell from.

> **Sales Person:** "John, your market is looking very competitive at the moment, before we look at anything else would you mind walking me through what you see as being the critical issues for your company in the next 12 months?"

✓ **Quick TIP**: For improved tone, hold the handset like a microphone when leaving voicemail.

Prospect: "Yeah, you're right, probably the key things for us are new sales growth, managing our costs, employee retention and new product development."

Sales Person: "...is there anything else?"

Prospect: "Well, I suppose compliance and regulation are going to have to be on the horizon"

Sales Person: "Of all those critical issues (showing list) what would you say has to be the #1 Priority?"

Prospect: "Hmmm ...If I had to chose one, well I suppose it would have to be New Product Development."

Sales Person: "Why did you choose that one?"

Prospect: "Over the past few years we have neglected this area and our competition have really gained a lot at our expense. I feel that it is essential for us to ramp this up now."

Sales Person: "Why is that important to YOU?"

Prospect: "When I started here I was proud of our products, we were the clear market leaders. A lot of our newer staff have never had that feeling. It would be great to see that back again."

Sales Person: "So what would be the consequences of this not being fixed?"

Prospect: "Well we would probably lose more Market share and $$$ and look pretty much like this years performance."

Sales Person: "Why would that worry you?"

> **Prospect:** "My CEO has promised the board and shareholders that we shall be back in either the #1 or 2 spot in 18 months, a large part of my job is making that happen."

The only way this technique is going to help you is if you USE it. Before you walk into your next sales presentation say to yourself; "How do I **PREPARE** to sell?" Use the simple structure I have outlined in this book. Train with your colleagues using specific environments and relevant challenges.

If it is scarce, it MUST be good

I would like you to think about you and your product / service in relation to either perceived or real scarcity. Unless your prospect believes that they need to act NOW you will find it very difficult to move the sale process towards a close. The easiest way to see how this rule works is to take a look around in shop windows and the media;

- 'Limited Time Only'
- 'Only 10 Places left'
- 'Never to be Repeated'

Those of you who have children may recognize that this technique has been adopted by photographers. A photographer comes to your child's school and takes 10 pictures of your child. The first you hear of it is when they send you one (small) copy of each print and ask you to choose the ones you like and how many prints and sizes you want.

Now, if they have done a good job you might be interested, but what really works for them is saying you had better order plenty before a certain date as they regularly destroy all the negatives! Not many parents resist that call to action! The thought of those cute pictures being shredded forever is too much!

How can you use this? I suggest you take a clean piece of paper and on one side write a list of the various features of your product or service. Now spend a few minutes thinking about each one and how the scarcity rule could apply to it. These may be different for each customer but make a note because they are sales pressure points and if you understand your prospect and present correctly, they will greatly enhance your sales prospects.

This can also work in reverse. If your prospect believes that you have a deadline, or any inflexible commitment, and they are either the only or one of a limited number of potential customers, then the pressure will be on you to discount or 'value add'. In sales negotiation skills the #1 negotiation technique is: CONTINUOUS PROSPECTING. If you have an abundance of potential customers then you won't have to discount.

You are the product

☑ In an earlier tip *(Page 34)*, I asked you to make a list of the features of your product or service and build the perception of scarcity around each one. What I would like you to do now is change the focus from your product or service to you.

Roger Dawson, in his book *'The Secrets of Power Persuasion'*, has a useful exercise that I would encourage you to perform. It is quite simple. On a clean sheet of paper write down THREE ways that your customers could be rewarded for doing business with you.

After you have done this, look at your responses. Were any of the three similar to this;

"They are rewarded because they get me!"

Dawson says, and I agree with him, that this should really be a major reason for your customers to buy from or through you. What can you do today to ensure your customers feel this way?

Do your homework

If you are prospecting for large sales, then it is essential that you do some pre-work and research before you first call the PA, Secretary or Assistant to the key decision maker. Think about it, if your reason for calling, when you are speaking to the initial gatekeeper, is that you have 'Critical' or 'Important' information, you won't get through, you will just burn good opportunities, and feel frustrated and stressed.

Gatekeepers (think of them as the Gate KEY PERSON), hear this stuff ALL the time. You need to build your credibility with them. To do that you have to do some homework. What do I mean? Ok, obviously there is Trade Press, Magazines, the Internet, other media, and all the info your competition has access to.

My favorite way of getting valuable and relevant information is to call into the sales floor of my prospect's business, then explain to a fellow sales person what I am trying to do. Either ask for their help or for someone they think could help me.

Now when you call the gatekeeper, you will have a clearer understanding of the broader issues in the company AND the specific name of some one in THEIR company that you were speaking to earlier. Building this into your opening statement will greatly improve your contact rate with key decision makers.

'Yes' lives in the land of NO

If you are a professional sales person then you know that you are in the rejection business. The fact is that when prospecting, generally speaking more people will say NO to you rather than yes. As our experience grows and our skills develop we can have an impact on the ratio, but the key factor is that to thrive we NEED those rejections.

I heard the phrase above ('yes lives in the land of no') at a conference a few years ago and it has stayed with me ever since. I hope it makes as much sense and is as much help to you as it was to me.

What being 'professional' really means

I regularly talk and write about the need for all sales people to treat what they do and how they do it in a 'professional' manner. I thought I would expand on this critical understanding.

The most important distinction to make is that there are two different types of 'Professional'. There are 'Professional salespeople' and there are Professionals who sell. Depending on your market and environment you probably operate in one mode. I believe there is a place for both types and I also believe that we can operate in both modes. The key issue is that YOU are conscious of whether you are operating as a sales professional or a professional who sells at that time. Let's take a look at each of these.

Professional sales people are the more common type of the two executives. They tend to be well trained and schooled in sales methodology and practice. They are sales people FIRST and have taken responsibility for their own ability, development and success in a professional manner.

These skills and knowledge are then used in their place of work, whether they are selling classified advertising, real estate, motor vehicles or holidays. A few key industry words may be different but the techniques and 'structure' of the sales process could be identical.

On the other hand, 'Professionals who Sell' suggests that they are professionals FIRST and then sales people. What I mean by this is that they seek to discover customer needs and issues, which may not have even been recognized by the client. If after consultation and analysis, they cannot find a real need or if they know a better solution they will recommend the action which best suits the CLIENT, not the sales person or the employer organization.

If you are in a sales role with NO ongoing relationships or account management / business development, such as a third party telemarketing environment, then it is probable that the environment is one of transaction and process / technique only, Professional Selling.

The difference between the two styles is NOT about technique, it is about the length of the relationship with the client. Professionals who sell tend to 'walk away' from potential business if they cannot satisfy the REAL needs for their client. It is a subtle difference but whether you decide to operate as a professional who sells, or a sales professional your career and success will benefit.

The ten minute rule

There are many things we all HATE doing. If you are like me and are like most typical sales people then paperwork, administration and writing reports are up there in your top 10 list of pet hates. Here is a method I use which helps me to do those things.

I was born and grew up in Northern Ireland and I remember people would proudly tell any one who would listen that we had the highest rate of heart disease in the world! I think this had something to do with generations of fried food, Guinness and sitting in pubs all day smoking untipped cigarettes! Like many of my peers I was smoking 10 a day from the age of 10 and 20 by my 20th birthday.

I haven't had a cigarette now for over 15 years but even though I haven't smoked, I am still a smoker. The secret of my success?

I gave up by not giving up. I just extended the 'gaps' between cigarettes. I used the 10-minute rule. Every time I had the urge to smoke I would say to myself that I could have one in 10 minutes. But it had to be EXACTLY 10 minutes. If I missed it (which I did most of the time) I would have to wait another 10 minutes. Before long it was an hour and increasing between each ACTUAL cigarette. Now I use this rule and you can too, to get a handle on paperwork or any habit you want to create or destroy.

The next time something important needs doing and you have the sense you are procrastinating, just tell yourself that you can stop after 10 minutes. You will be surprised at how this little rule can bring big results in many areas of your life.

Less thought more action

Too many sales people spend too much time THINKING and not enough time DOING. If you find yourself or your colleagues constantly trying to come up with new and 'clever' ways of marketing your products and services to make the sale, I can almost guarantee that although you are being busy, you are really avoiding the basics.

Often the real solution to improving a slow or sluggish sales environment is less thought and more action. Are your quantity of calls / contacts with potential customers where they should be? Is your 'sensory acuity' tuned in to hear your prospect's needs and issues and to respond correctly?

Sales campaign planning is essential but it needs to be conducted outside 'selling' time and adjusted frequently. After this your prospecting activities can be measured.

Sensory Acuity is a valuable asset we all possess. Correctly managed it enables us to 'sense' or pick up often hidden emotive indicators such as nervousness, concern, reservations etc.

Trust your activity. The more you prospect, the better you will get.

Qualify quicker and make your sales bigger!

How many meetings, sales calls and phone calls should you have with a client before you call it a day and move on? An error I often see a lot of sales people making is to keep selling to a 'prospect' until they either say yes or no. Now persistence does pay, however not as well as qualifying early and closing correctly.

You need to have a rough idea of how many phone calls, visits and 'proposals' and TIME you are prepared to commit for a certain sale amount. If you are not prepared to STOP selling to that prospect and move on, you will end up with a diary which is full of meetings, stress and little to NO cash.

Of course more effort is sometimes required for larger and more complex sales and negotiations but you still need to have a value on your time and involvement. Let your prospect know that you have allocated a number of visits / calls and they will usually operate within your expectations.

It's time to wake up, shake up and SERVICE your prospects

Have you got a number of prospects sitting on proposals? You have covered everything with them and have 'exhausted' your reasons to call them to speed the process up?

You are not alone. This scenario is replicated in sales teams around the world. It can be even worse towards the end of the month / quarter. You have told your manager that you expected the deal to be closed and done by the end of the sales period, yet the client who promised to call you back with an answer, fax over the paperwork, e-mail you the order number etc is strangely silent.

You need to be careful in this type of scenario. If you call too much and you don't have a valid reason, you can spoil the deal. It is not good enough to call; 'just to see how things are' or ' to see if there has been any progress'. You appear over keen and 'junior'. It is also a stressful way to manage your sales environment and sales cycle.

The key here is to have a variety of reasons to contact. Reasons that are not connected to the proposed sale but ARE relevant and of interest to your prospect. Here are a few favorites of mine:

I was just thinking of you: At a function or event something comes to your attention that could be of value to your client and gives you a reason to call.

> "Mr Customer, I was at a business luncheon yesterday and the guest speaker mentioned something and I thought of you..."

Demonstrate Interest: If you come across relevant articles in business and trade press, tear them out and mail them with a short personal note:

> "I just read this article and thought of you.."

Make them the Hero: Think like you are their PR agent. Find a reason to get them / their angle / their opinion into a trade publication, or of interest to the media.

These strategies are not instant and require your ongoing attention. But if you have a number of clients with long sales cycles or are procrastinators, get active and develop a few ways to surprise and excite them with your next call.

Time Questions

If you are interested in becoming a more effective sales professional there are a couple of key questions you need to ask yourself on a regular basis.

1. What am I doing wrong that I can stop?
2. What am I doing right so I can continue?
3. What am I NOT doing that I should start?
4. How can I measure my progress on an ongoing basis?

Each day examine your activity and remind yourself to continually revise your methods and practices.

'Danger, danger, Will Robinson...'

If you watched the series or saw the movie 'Lost In Space' produced some years ago you may remember the robot. Whenever Will Robinson, the boy in the family, encountered any danger, his trusty robot would alert him and the family by loudly blaring; 'Danger, Danger'.

As a professional I have often been in danger of wasting my time when I think I am being productive, that's when we all need some sort of 'Mental' robot which starts signalling the danger ahead and allows us the opportunity to recover. A danger I want to alert you to is the 'long conversation'. When a prospect on a call says; '…tell me more about that' or something similar. This can be music to our ears. We can easily slip into long phone presentations / conversations which are using more time than they really deserve.

Avoid long conversations. If a prospect asks a question or sends a buying signal, use that as a reason to 'close' the appointment or the sale right there. If they are truly interested they will agree with you, if not, move on!

No thanks, we're happy with our current supplier

The vast majority of your prospects already have an ongoing relationship with one of your competitors and will often say 'no thanks we're happy with our current supplier'. Once you recognize this, you have to KNOW how to deal with this objection.

First of all, realize that it is highly unlikely that what you say in response to this objection is going to make your prospect do a 180-degree turn.

Try the following: Congratulate them and ask what is it that their supplier does so well. When they have answered (don't debate them!) ask them what they think they could improve on.

Make notes of all their comments and call back in a few days / weeks. Open the conversation with something along the lines of;

> "I have been thinking about what you said and it occurred to me that…"

Negotiating is NOT selling

☑ There is a huge difference between selling and negotiating. The two are not the same and although traditionally you may have been conditioned to think they are, the sooner you split the two disciplines, the sooner you can start to become more successful.

When the railway, shipping or transport unions go on strike; when criminals take hostages; when other conflicts erupt governments don't rush off and send in teams of sales people, they send in trained negotiators.

I recommend that you spend time and energy improving your negotiating skills. They are a valuable component in any sale. Here are a couple of key principles that can easily be incorporated into your current sales methodology.

You need to ask for more than you expect

The key word here is YOU. Too often salespeople actually devalue their own product or service before they go into a sales environment. It is really quite simple, why should I as a buyer pay more for your product than YOU believe it is worth. The solution is to understand the value of the outcome that your product will provide for your prospect.

Trade all concessions

Make sure that if you do make a concession that it is reciprocal. That means making sure your prospect gives you leads, referrals, a longer contract, exclusivity or something of value EACH time.

Never say YES to the first offer

Have you ever offered a salesperson a price and they said YES too quickly and a little too enthusiastically? Perhaps it left you with a feeling that your price was a little too generous. The lesson here is that if you are the sales person, make sure that your prospect feels that you are giving the offer serious consideration.

Feel, felt, found

One of THE classic objection handling techniques if not the #1 is the 'feel, felt, found' strategy. Most sales people have come across this before but cannot recall it when they need it. I find it particularly useful when a prospect throws an objection I have not heard before and am not fully prepared to deal with.

Here is an example scenario to illustrate how it works:

> **Prospect:** "We have no spare time to run this type of initiative".

This really could apply to anything. Our sales person, even though they have never heard this objection before, can respond without hesitating.

> **Sales Person:** "I know how you **FEEL**, many of what are now my best customers also **FELT** like that when we started looking at this, but then they **FOUND** that our unique (feature) helped them not only reduce waste but actually increase available resources."

The first stage (I know how you FEEL) establishes empathy with your prospect. The second stage (many of my best customers also FELT) establishes that they are not alone and others have gone through this process. Finally, (they FOUND), is suggesting or demonstrating that there is evidence or proof of your product / service's success with other equally sceptic prospects. This technique should be an absolute essential tool in your sales 'kit'. Use it today.

What do your customers tell you?...

A great phrase to build into your opening statements or as part of your objection handling process is "...Our customers tell us we have the best prices." or "our customers tell us that our service is the best they've found". Another version would be; "our customers tell us that our product / service is the best they have ever used".

Each one of these is focused on the three key elements of any product or service: The product *quality*, the customer *service* and the *price*. The next time you are speaking to one of your loyal customers ask them why they chose to use you. Once they respond, you will feel more comfortable about using the phrase to give your own testimonials during prospecting sessions. This is even more powerful if your customer is prepared to give you a written testimonial.

No hang ups

When I am making prospecting calls, I try to hang up as little as possible between calls.

Now it is critical that you review your call immediately after it ends but too many sales people take too long to do this and they 'over analyze' and vastly slow down their calling quantity. To fix this I recommend that you don't hang up, keep the phone in your hand. This puts pressure on you to act quickly and move on to the next call. In those few seconds identify the strengths and weaknesses in your performance and what you should stop or improve on.

Then in your next call apply what you learned straight away. Using this, you not only make better calls but your prospecting figures will rocket!

Treat different customers differently

Have you ever spent time thinking about why it is that you 'get on' better with some people and not with others? I am sure that you can think of a couple of clients or prospects that make you wonder how anyone could get on with them and yet many others do.

Our customers are left with an impression of us when we interact with them either on the phone or in face-to-face sales meetings. Many organizations use various profiling tools such as MBTI and DISC that were all developed based on the original work of Carl Jung, the Swiss psychologist, who developed a personality typology.

As sales people we normally don't have the time to conduct personality analyses of our customers in depth. I found that I needed something quick and simple, a 'ready reckoner' I could use easily and quickly.

There are four key types of prospects that you are going to meet / talk to on a regular basis. Knowing how to change and adapt your presentation and language for each will help you build rapport and create a platform from which to sell successfully. Let's quickly look at each one separately.

Producers

Bottom line focused and performance driven, Producers have a 'now' focus and can be impatient and quite directive in their language. When you are selling to Producers you have to present the benefits of your product (in their language) up front. They like to be in control and can appear to be uncaring or dismissive. They are hard to get hold of, so you need to be persistent and be ready to respond quickly and with confidence.

Processors

Analytical and process driven individuals. To many sales people they can appear overly cautious and slow, although what they are really searching for is independent proof / evidence of your claim statement. So when selling to Processors, your recommendations should be at the END and your language should be full of reason, facts, logic and proof. Make your case overwhelming, invite their own independent assessment. Illustrate other happy customers with referrals and testimonials.

Proactive

We all know somebody like this, a lot of sales people fall into this category. They love ideas and innovation, anything that is new to take to the market. But on the other hand they hate paperwork and administration. Proactives tend to get motivated and distracted easily and find it difficult to stick to plans / agendas and commitments. If you are selling to a proactive person change your language to a 'future focus', what the benefits will be like. Involve them, solicit their opinion and give them a sense of ownership of the 'idea'.

Protectors

Protectors are motivated by community, team and a sense of relationship. A lot of gatekeepers are protectors as are people in many service professions like teachers, nurses etc. These individuals are the emotional 'glue' that holds together business units. They tend to be the people who organize office birthdays, social outings etc.

So when you are approaching a protector, empathize with them and adjust your opening statement to demonstrate how your product / service will 'help' the team to remove or reduce any risk. A relaxed tone will help gain their trust.

I have only touched the surface of this fascinating area. The truth is that none of us are 100% one or the other. We are a combination of the four, with a preference (in certain conditions) to behave or act in a certain way. Out of the work environment, many people behave and interact with others very differently.

One of the most dangerous things you can do is to assume that your prospects / customers have a fixed position. The method to make sure your current analysis is correct is with good diagnostic questioning and listening techniques.

So what?

For many sales people it is all too easy to discuss / talk at length about what we think are our wonderful products and services. We can bore our prospects, their eyes glaze over and their jaws slacken. Our prospect only has to ask us a question, which we see as a flashing neon buying signal, saying TALK, TALK, TALK about our product!

There is a wonderful and simple technique we can use which not only prevents us rambling on and losing our prospect's attention, but ensures that what we do say is related back to them and their needs. The next time you are in front of a prospect, I want you to imagine that the words 'So What?' are painted on their forehead. This probably represents what they are really thinking most of the time you are talking.

Every time you mention a feature or illustrate a generic benefit it will remind you to add the words: 'so what that means for you is…' by adding these words you will be forced to tie in your benefit statement to them specifically.

Ps - where's your V Card?

When you send an e-mail to a prospect or customer, there are a couple of things to remember:

Include a 'V' CARD. A 'V' Card is an electronic business card. By including one, each time you send an e-mail, your contact has the option of automatically including your business card in their database. You only have to do it once, and then it is included as a small attachment. To do this in

Outlook, go to: Tools ▶ Options ▶ Mail ▶ format and follow the prompts in signatures.

Sign Off: While you are there, make sure your name and contact details are included in the **sign off** text of each e-mail by setting it up permanently.

Have a PS line. Research shows that people read the headline and 'P.S.' line in correspondence first. So include a 'P.S.' line in each e-mail directing prospects to a special offer or promotion.

Telephone 'PIPS'

I have frequently highlighted the importance of the tonality of your voice to convey, authority, sincerity and confidence. When you are on the telephone this is even more critical. 85% of the impression your prospects will have after and during your call will be based on the tone of your voice, so it makes sense to get it right. There are four key elements in creating a positive telephone image. I call these the 'PIPS'.

PAUSE: Deliberately pause for slightly longer than you feel comfortable, it gives your prospect time to think.

INFLECTION: Make sure you do not have a rising inflection at the end of phrases or sentences, it sounds like a request.

PACE: Match the pace of your subject's language, slow down or speed up as necessary.

SELF CONFIDENCE: Make sure you sound confident by recording and rehearsing key phrases until they sound just right.

If you haven't got the time to do it right – when will you find the time to do it over?

This is a great question. Jeffrey Mayer deals with it in his book of the same title. There are plenty of time management books and programs in the market, most of them are generic and very few are related specifically to the sales environment. Having read most of them, here are some of my key observations for sales people:

- Make prospecting for NEW business the first thing you do every day.
- Delegate to yourself; allocate times for administration and paperwork out of key contact time.
- Don't go to meetings unless you know why and how they can help you.
- Ask yourself what would happen if you did nothing about a task, if you cannot think of a consequence, then dump it
- Create goals on a monthly campaign basis. Create your to-do list and plan on a weekly basis. Change tactics on a daily basis.
- Get Help; get an assistant or assistance so that your workload is being managed while you are selling.

'Own' the building, street, suburb..........

A simple but extremely effective strategy is simply contacting the other businesses in your building and letting them know you exist. You can extend this strategy to all the other businesses surrounding your client's building / office / street.

Here is how it works. If ABC enterprises are a customer or even a prospect, you have a great reason to contact all the other offices in that building. Don't try to sell them on the phone, just sell the appointment.

> **For example:** "Mr Jones, John Doe here from XYZ and Co, the reason for my call today is that we have just competed a (project / installation / analysis) for a neighbor of yours, Jane Smith at 123. We were able to not only reduce their costs and paperwork, but also at the same time actually double their performance and handling. I am visiting Jane next week and while I am there I would love to call by and show you how we did this. Is Tuesday or Wednesday best for you?"

The key here is not only building a contact list from your existing clients, but having a great opening statement which reduces their Pain and increases the Gain.

Be consistent

This appears to be almost like a law of human nature. We all prefer consistency in our lives. Our customers and prospects want things to work the same way every time they happen.

When they wake up in the morning they want to find the floor under their feet, the sun above their heads and coffee in their cups. Just as they expect physical consistency, they also expect psychological consistency. If they have marriages, families, and jobs yesterday, they expect to find them today in pretty much the same condition.

Thus, our prospects have 'mental worlds' of expectations, the people in them, and their relationships. On your first call you are interrupting this world, YOU are the inconsistency. So how can your product or service help them remain consistent? How can you demonstrate that? If you can demonstrate an existing relationship with a colleague of theirs or an authority they respect, then consistency becomes like a form of human gravity.

To become a welcome interruption you need to focus on **THEIR** issues.

How to write a great elevator speech

Let's imagine for a moment that you have just walked into a premium office building in the CBD. You are on your way up to the seventeenth floor to visit a prospect and present to them your thoughts and ideas. You are excited about this meeting, as you have been working on securing an appointment for months.

As you get into the lift an imposing figure jumps in at the last moment just before the doors close. You recognize him from the annual report and website as the chairman of the company and you both exchange polite greetings, he notices your name badge you were given at reception and asks the following question:

    "So, John what do you do?"

✓ **Quick TIP**: The first objection is usually false – your target is to get to the third or fourth.

This is the moment of truth. The 'Elevator Pitch'! This is the moment you will either deliver a vague, forgettable and 'corporate' phrase, or a short succinct and compelling response which invites your lift colleague to engage further.

Most sales people rely on their corporate slogans or marketing positioning statements and / or are guilty of 'mms' and 'ahhs', mumbling and making the prospect wish they had never asked.

Although a cliché, the concept of an elevator speech, pitch or presentation works because you have about 15 – 20 seconds to deliver. This does not mean cramming in more words for greater impact. It does however mean thinking ahead, writing and editing and rehearsing until your response becomes second nature.

There are a couple of outcomes you should ensure in your elevator speech:

1. It and your delivery are memorable (this helps you AND them).
2. Talk about results, not fluff
3. Focus on your target's benefits
4. Almost always create an inquisitive response ('Oh how did you do that?')

There is a great deal more detail behind really great elevator speeches, but the most simple way to build one is a three step format:

1. I / we help,
2. By.....,
3. So that...

For example in response to; So what do you do? A response could be:

> "I help sales managers and sales people perform better by motivating and training them so that they are in control and on top of their budgets"

If I wanted to get a little bit more creative with my CEO in the lift I could say;

> "I help CEO's and senior managers sleep better at night by making sure their sales teams are on top of their game and winning more than their fair share of business".

> The response you should be aiming for is a question like; "How do you do that?" You can then build a discussion from a solid platform.

Managing the 'Not interested' response

Have you ever sold a product or service to someone who was initially uninterested? I'm sure that you have, in fact it is likely that ALL prospects have this response / objection before we call them. It is only logical because if they were interested they would have called us first, right?

The first and most important key to managing this is managing your own predisposition towards it. It is really just a 'knee jerk' reaction rather than a true reflection of your prospect's real objection. When you realize that you have overcome it before, many times before, then it is much easier to deal with and overcome.

Personally, in this situation I like to use the 'Feel, Felt, Found' technique *(see page 46)*. Another favorite of mine is R.U.S.T *(see page 116);* "Are you just saying that (to get me off the phone)?" You would be amazed at how many people say yes to this and then give me another, more valid objection. More on this later in the book.

Voicemail

Leaving voice mail is a fact of life in business sales. If you ignore it and leave no message I can guarantee that you are losing business because of it. Do NOT give them your life story. The purpose of leaving a vm (voicemail) is so they WANT to call you back. Here is one way of achieving this.

> **Name Dropping**; "John, it's Peter Sells here from World's Best Widgets; my number is 9222 9112, could you call me back, it's regarding Fred Bloggs" (Fred's name should be known by the prospect).

That is it, no more detail, if they want detail, they can call me back. Of course when they do call, I can use an opening statement, which incorporates and legitimizes the relevance of Fred.

In the same way you can use company names and brands to create their interest. Just remember it is critical that you have planned out your rationale and why this should be of interest / value to your prospect BEFORE your speak to them.

THE WORLD'S BEST SALES TIPS

Train yourself!

If I were to ask you right now what type of self-development program you were currently working on, what would you truly say? Most sales people NEVER attend or invest in their own development in any way, and they are constantly struggling with budgets / managers and mediocre performances.

So, where do you begin? Are you a member of a local sales networking club? If not go to your local phone directory or Google and find a local organization and pick up the phone, it's a great way to network and build your skills.

Do you realize that of the 100% of people who buy 'How to…' type books / tapes and cds only 10% actually get to the end of the book! If that was not bad enough only 10% of that group (1%) actually change their behavior and put what they have learned / read / watched into practice.

Why is that? It is easy to get the sense of commitment when we make the investment and buy that $25.00 book and walk out of the store feeling empowered, but have a look around your bookshelves. I bet that right now you have got enough material and content on hand to dramatically change your business / life for the better if only you had read them and acted on the advice you had already invested in.

Showroom sales – show me the money!

Some of the best sales professionals you are ever likely to meet are in 'retail' businesses where professionals do most of their selling on a showroom floor. This was reinforced to me recently when I observed a salesman in action at a popular white goods retailer. On the showroom floor I could see a couple that were interested in a particularly large fridge with a big red 'SALE' sticker on the front. I was pretended to be looking at air conditioners and kept myself in the background, close enough to hear everything.

They were opening the door, looking at the shelves etc. they even had a tape measure and were 'measuring up' to see if the fridge would fit. Now in any salesperson's mind they would have to qualify as interested prospects. This became really interesting when I observed the sales person do something unusual. Rather than just go over and ask 'can I help you' or the clichéd ; "If you need anything..." this professional used a great technique which closed the sale in moments.

First of all he allowed the couple to spend time with the fridge, building their sense of ownership through their senses (sight, touch, sound) and discussing it with each other. When he felt that the time was right he approached the couple and said;

> "I can understand why you are interested in this particular model. At this price it is fantastic value, (slight pause) but I am pretty sure we sold the last one earlier this morning."

At this point it was obvious to see the disappointment in the faces of the couple. Remember at this point there had been NO conversation. The sales person had simply approached the couple and said a few sentences. The impact of his language on them however was immediate. After a couple of quick glances at each other, they asked if it were likely that there were any others in the storeroom or at another franchise. The sales person 'flinched' slightly and then closed them by saying:

> "I would be happy to get on the phone and check around for you, but do I understand that if I find a shop which does have one at this price, you'll take it?"

You've guessed it, the sales person came back a few minutes later with the good news and an order form. Now why would a sales person do this? You could argue that the couple were going to buy anyway. Indeed they may have done so, after haggling on the price and wasting the sales person's time.

Because the fridge suddenly became scarce and potentially unavailable, it became much more desirable. If there were 40 of them on the showroom floor I don't imagine there would have been the same sense of urgency. You can adapt this strategy to fit your business.

Would you like $86,400?

Imagine for a moment that every morning when you wake up, a secret benefactor makes a deposit of $86,400 into your bank account. There is only one catch; each day, anything that you have NOT spent will be taken from you. Now if you knew that this was going to happen each day, what would you do?

When I ask participants this question, no one hesitates, the answers are always the same, spend everything and make sure there is not one cent left in the bank! Have you guessed what the metaphor is? There are 86,400 seconds in every day and each one vanishes forever. We need to make the most of the limited time we have available, yet many of us will procrastinate and waste time. You can't waste anyone's time but your own.

The real key is to spend your time wisely on activities that will 'compound' over time and deliver ongoing benefits. What would happen to your sales if you did a fantastic job for your top 20 clients rather than a mediocre one for 200 of them?

Avoid equal sized concessions

☑ One of my key principles of negotiating is, CONTINUOUS PROSPECTING. If you have a surplus of prospects there is much less pressure on you to negotiate. But there are going to be times when you are involved in a genuine negotiation. A genuine negotiation is one where both parties fundamentally want to do business with each other, they just need to agree on terms.

If you know that you have $5,000 'give' with which you are prepared to reduce your price, you need to be careful that you do not make equal sized concessions. The reason is obvious, even if you are trading concessions, your prospect will quickly realize that every concession moves in say $500 increments and they will expect each concession to be at least that large.

By varying the concession and relating it to the VALUE of the reciprocal concession you will keep your prospect and yourself focused on closing the deal and moving forward.

Indifferent? who cares?

What is the opposite of customer dissatisfaction? When I ask that question at conferences, seminars and training programs most people give me the right answer; The opposite of customer dissatisfaction is customer satisfaction! When I ask how do you change unhappy customers into happy ones again lots of good and valid strategies come up; exceeding their expectations, great service, listening and engaging.

Most organizations 'satisfied' customers are neither satisfied or dissatisfied. They are simply indifferent. This is potentially lethal because the company has the illusion they are doing a good job. All that is required is for another provider to tip the balance in their favor very slightly and they will be out of business.

They are neither happy nor unhappy, we think we have repaired the damage, but the truth is they could be 'poached' by a competitor easily. Only 20% of what you think of as you most loyal customers actually ARE. The only way to stay on top of this is by constantly 'delighting' your customers.

On-going, in-depth qualitative research into your marketplace and 'warts and all' honesty is the way to ensure that your product / service will truly exceed expectations and remain competitive in the medium / long term.

If you haven't got a plan - you're a tourist!

I was speaking at an industry sales seminar recently where most of the participants were directors / owners of their own businesses. Early in my presentation, I asked the audience this question;

> "Give me an idea of what I'm working with here, how many of you have a sales plan?"

As you might have expected over 90% of the audience raised their hand. I then asked the audience another question:

> "Of those who have a sales plan, how many of your plans are really nothing more than last year's results with X% added on?"

As I expected, rather sheepishly most people kept their hands in the air. Everyone knew they were kidding themselves! Stop and think for a moment, do YOU have a plan? Most organizations do not have a sales plan, they do have a revenue goal and their strategy is pretty much do what we did last year and 'hope' that a couple of new pieces of business will come in or the 'market' picks up.

If you haven't got a sales plan you're a sales tourist. Whether you are the Managing Director or a new sales executive you are just visiting and having a 'look' around! I would encourage you to take responsibility for your plan. Even if your manager / boss / company has a plan, you still need to make your own.

Here are a few tips for creating a successful sales plan

- Budget **ACTIVITY** first, before dollars

- Prioritize key accounts and relationships by revenue and 'leverage'
- Plan only 3 - 4 'core' goals weekly
- Measure and adjust activity daily (effort and focus)
- Be prepared to dump bottom 15 - 20% clients
- Have some allowance for unforeseen 'disasters' (you lose two of your top five accounts)

"With a plan like this, you are doing your competition a favor!"

A good sales plan has to be a resource for you and others who use it. It has to be about 'how' you will achieve. I like to think of it as a future diary. Of course, the chance of the final outcome following your script is unlikely, but that's not the point. The point is that you have a methodology that over time you can control, refine, and calibrate.

Finally, a good plan involves YOUR development as the key resource to deliver the outcome. It should honestly evaluate your strengths and weaknesses and include development activities to minimize and enhance your capability.

Look into my eyes…

I remember playing the stare game in school, two people keep eye contact and the first person to blink loses! Often in a negotiation or sales interview, your prospect can try and intimidate you with a continuous gaze. It's not quite a 'blinking contest', but it is not far off. For novice and inexperienced sales people, this can take you off guard and 'throw' your focus and concentration.

I'm sure you have had a conversation with someone who is avoiding your eye contact. For most of us avoiding eye contact is not good for building trust and rapport. So as confident sales professionals, we need a simple way to maintain eye contact without staring at our prospect.

If you are uncomfortable with this level of intense eye contact then the best way to avoid this is to look steadily at their forehead. At a normal distance (table width apart), your prospect will not be able to notice that you are not staring back but will feel as if you are meeting their direct gaze.

When your mutual gaze breaks below eye level a more social atmosphere quickly develops.

I'm at the airport

I can't say I know exactly why it works, but when I leave voice mail messages for hard to reach prospects from the airport, by the time the plane lands I usually have a message from them returning my call! My message is simple, I don't give away too much information; I leave a reference and I mention that I am calling from the airport.

One reason I suspect that it works is that my prospect feels more comfortable because they can ring and KNOW I won't answer! Because my message deliberately did not give too much away, almost 90% of them give me permission to call them back with their direct or mobile number!

I would like you to try this yourself. If you are traveling in the next couple of weeks, build a list of 10 to 20 hard to reach prospects and call them before you board. Leave a tight voice mail, make sure you tell them you are calling from the airport and turn your phone off.

How do I sound?

I believe this is THE single most powerful and easiest way to take control and immediately improve your sales prospecting performance.

What is this magic method? It is so simple and so cheap. For about $50.00 you can buy a simple micro cassette hand held tape recorder. With a couple of AA batteries and a phone hook up, you can record your opening pitches and how you deal with objections (check you local laws prior).

✓ **Quick TIP**: Present your weakest case first – it builds more credibility with the prospect.

Everybody cringes when they hear themselves on tape, but that is the reality. Just by listening you will adjust your tone pitch and success rate!

Give me back that proposal!

Have you ever been involved in a presentation to a client when you lost control. I don't mean 'flipped'. What I am referring to is when YOUR sales presentation is taken over by the prospect. How could something like this happen and more importantly what can you do as a professional to regain control.

Let's imagine the following scenario. There are only the two of you in the room. Your 'presentation' is across a table and is based on a document / proposal you have created specifically for this client. A typical sales presentation in many office environments is semi-formal. A few minutes into the delivery, for whatever reason, the prospect picks up a copy of the proposal. You are now officially in sales trouble!

Three things tend to happen here:

- **You lose eye contact with your prospect**
- **They start flicking the pages and reading your proposal**
- **Your discomfort level increases to match your lack of control**

To make matters worse, you could be dealing with a 'Producer' type personality *(see page 49)*. They will probably flick right to the back page, look at your costing or investment schedule and give an obvious 'flinch' *(see page 8)*. Suddenly you've been put on the back foot with a focus on your PRICE rather than VALUE!

Before we discuss what to do / not to do to prepare for this type of presentation, here is a simple and effective way to RECOVER control when this happens.

Stop presenting / talking while they are reading. Wait for your prospect to ask a question. Do not answer, but look slightly puzzled. Then mention that the point / answer is in the proposal somewhere, you're not quite sure where. While at the same time extending your hand, gesturing for the return of the document. They will generally hand it back to you. You can then give it a glance yourself, respond to the question and proceed with your presentation while placing the proposal firmly under your elbow!

Of course the best way to handle this is to not let it happen at all. Generally there are three parts to any presentation; the document, which is a leave behind, the delivery which are your words, gestures and performance. And the visual element whether PowerPoint, flipcharts, notepaper or simply your physiology.

A final note, I would recommend that you do not forward your sales presentation to the prospect. I have met puzzled sales executives who are wondering why their 'hot' prospect called canceling their appointment after they had emailed their proposal!

Scribbled proposals

Here is a tip that can help your proposal work for you once you have left it with the prospect, and ensure that it sells for you.

Do you remember when you were at school and the teacher returned your homework the next day? There would be correction marks and comments in red ink in the margins. Perhaps even a few notes and highlighted sections. When you produce your next proposal document, I want you to go over it and highlight key points, write your thoughts in the margins, use arrows to direct their attention, even stick a few post it notes.

This should not be overly 'neat'. The impact of this 'tailoring' is a document that still lives after you are gone. Your prospect's attention will unconsciously be drawn to the highlighted areas when they review it.

Also, should it ever be distributed to others, they may assume the comments came from their colleague! Find an old proposal on your computer and trial this to see how good it looks.

'RUST' never sleeps

I wish I could guarantee that ALL my readers were keen prospectors and made their call quota each day. I suspect though, that you are not as attentive as I would like! Here is a magical little technique that just knocks down flat the first objection you hear from a prospect on a cold call. In my experience, it is usually the third or even the fourth objection that is actually real and needs to be dealt with. The first one is just to get you off the phone.

Too many sales people fall at this hurdle when they do not need to. So the next time you get a standard objection within seconds of your opening statement I want you to use the '**RUST**' technique (R U just Saying That).

Your prospect says, "sorry not interested!" With a little humour in the tone of your voice I want you to say; "Are you just saying that to get me off the phone?" and then shut up. In nine out of 10 cases, your prospect will laugh and say yes! They will then give you another objection such as, "but really we have spent our budget". You can now deal with the second objection. More on RUST later in the book *(see page 116)*.

Are you an expert of choice?

Think about if for a moment. If one of your customers was listing the pros and cons of you versus your competitors, what could they know about you personally which would make you their expert of choice?

This fundamentally addresses the issue that is one of the major reasons why your customers choose to do business with you. It is not because of your organization it is because of YOU. All our clients can get competitive products and services from a variety of sources, but when you differentiate your offering by recognizing that your relationship IS part of the overall customer experience, you are forced to constantly improve and exceed their and your expectations.

I believe that it is critical that you position yourself as an **'Expert of Choice'** in each of your client's mindsets.

Sounds interesting

What do you think is the single biggest mistake salespeople make when they are calling for new business on the phone? In my experience it is that they have an opening statement that builds RESISTANCE rather than INTEREST! It sounds obvious, doesn't it?

Imagine this scenario; you have come home from a days work and as soon as you are through the door the phone rings. Before you even know who it is, you have already decided that you do not want to speak to them. The feeling is compounded when you realise it is someone calling you about a 'great opportunity' in timeshare, wine clubs, holiday packages and more! When you are making a prospective call it is critical that you realize that you are interrupting. Your prospect was quite happily going about their routine. You stopped that and worse still, probably sounded like you were trying to sell something!

So what should you do? What is the correct way to approach this? How do we create a winning script? In previous tips and hints I have touched on this critical aspect for your prospecting success. In this tip I want to expand on that and give you some specific elements which will greatly enhance your success rate.

First things first, our initial outcome from our opening statement is NOT to sell, it has to be to generate a positive response in their mind. The words I want the prospect to be thinking immediately after my short opening statement are; "sounds interesting". Now they are probably NOT going to say that out loud but that is my clear goal. I know I have achieved this when they ask me a question (buying signal).

There is a 'formula' or method for creating opening statements of interest that I have used and trained others in for years. It is not only easy to remember but simple to execute. Take this technique, practise it and make it your own.

1. Introduction and reason why calling
2. Some recent and relevant (to the prospect) successes
3. What you did to reduce (PAIN: what they want less of)
4. What you did to increase (GAIN: what they want more of)
5. Next step with alternative choice

Here's an example;

> "Mr Jones, My name is Peter Sells of World's Best Widgets. I wanted to speak with you today because recently we have been having a great deal of success with other companies in your industry, helping them not only reduce the time and frustration in getting more activity from their sales teams, but at the same time increasing the amount of NEW business and sales from their existing clients. I am in your (street, building, suburb) later this week and would love to show you how we did this. Would Thursday or Friday be a better day for you?"

For another look at this essential technique see page 1.

Reading 'windows'

When you sell to retailers it is always a good idea to spend some time 'reading' their shop window before walking in. More often than not there will a number of items on sale or a special offer which can give you valuable insight into the mind of the owner / manager.

You can employ the same strategy in an office environment even if they do not have shop-fronts in a traditional sense. There are two 'windows' I recommend; their website and believe it or not the prospect's desk and office.

Generally speaking most companies will have information on recent appointments, acquisitions, future growth strategies and historic performance on their website. All valuable information to help you build relevance of your product / service and interest from your prospect.

Your prospect's desk can tell you much about their personality, whether it is military like in its neatness and order, or it resembles a badly arranged haystack. For more insights into personality styles see page 48.

The power of testimonials

In previous tips I have written about why it is important that your prospects and clients believe that you are an 'Expert of Choice' *(see page 71)*. A question that would naturally flow from this could be: How do you become an expert of choice? Well, for starters do not do tell them that you are an expert! This can come across as a challenge.

They can choose whether to believe you or not and you can sound arrogant and aloof.

The easiest way to position yourself as an expert of choice is by offering PROOF, and the best form of proof is not what you say, but what your customers have said. So when you do a good job and the client has thanked you I suggest you ask them for a testimonial.

These letters, which you will collect each time, will add weight to your expertise. From your prospect's point of view the absolute best proof is of course word of mouth. This is because they are receiving the referral 'live' and from someone whom they trust. If you have any clients who are actively referring you, treat them like the valuable resource they are.

Leveraging your lists

How much time and effort do you and your organization spend creating and improving your prospect lists? Probably not much. A major factor in your success or failure on any sales campaign is the quality of the names and numbers you have in a database, 'tickle' file or printed list.

A complaint sales people often have is the poor quality of their list. Well, if you are not in a position to change your raw data (ie. buy your own list) then it is critical that you quickly go through your list and grade or prioritize those most likely to buy your product or service. On any one campaign you will probably need several thousand names and numbers and have a limited amount of time to get through to them.

Here is my suggestion. You need to spend a couple of hours every day dialling and delivering an opening statement which will allow your prospect to grade themselves as either interested or not. Develop those who are interested and 'drop' those who are not until you have gone through the whole list and secured all the initial interest. You can then recall your 'B' list.

Show me the value!

Here is a quick exercise for you. Get a clean sheet of paper and a pen. On one side of the paper write down the name of a typical product or service that you sell on a regular basis. For instance, for the home cleaning industry you might select 'carpet cleaning' or for retail banking you might select a 'variable mortgage' product. You get the idea, something that you sell frequently and easily.

Now, before you do anything else, write down the value of that product or service underneath. Take a moment and do this now.

When I facilitate this exercise in my training programs and seminars at least 70% of participants do the same thing. Perhaps you did also. I do know sales people and it is more than likely that you did not actually do the exercise above, but just read on. That's OK, but what was in your mind when I asked you to think about the value of your product or service? Most sales people write down the price. Some even write down the discounted price!

It's an easy mistake to make but it could be one that is costing you substantially. It is essential that you understand the huge difference between PRICE and

VALUE. Price is just a number which has been attached to your product / service. Value, on the other hand is something which varies from one prospect to the next and is up to you to investigate, discover and agree on, BEFORE you deal with price.

Let's look at an example. Let's imagine you are in newspaper advertising sales and a standard advertisement is $5,000. Now, your prospect sells luxury German cars which range in price from $60k to 400k. If you knew that from their last series of three advertisements (their investment = $15,000.) they received 20 sales leads and sold three vehicles totalling $250k, what is the VALUE of your advertisement now?

I can hear everyone saying, that prospects themselves don't know this most of the time and if they did they aren't going to volunteer this information! You're right, but you know what? As a professional sales person, it is YOUR job to discover the value of your solution for your prospect. Your prospects are happy for you to focus on price because then you can be negotiated as a commodity rather than as an asset. A simple way to discover your prospect's values would be to use my **'PREPARE'** questioning technique outlined earlier in the book *(see page 29)*.

List management

Before you purchase a mailing list or a cold calling list from a broker, always ask for a sample of roughly 5%. If your list was 5,000 sales managers in the CBD then I would want 250 as a sample to test the market prior to the full purchase. The sample should not be a 'chunk' but be as wide as possible, I suggest you chose a number such as every n'th where 'n' is for every fiftieth contact.

You of course pay for your sample, but rather than pay for a full 'dud' list and fail, you have the opportunity to adjust the campaign offer / style / delivery or reconfigure the list profile.

Often a phone campaign or a mail campaign will be greatly enhanced when BOTH mediums are used rather than relying on one exclusively. Follow up your mail out with a phone call. Any calls which did not progress should be followed up with a postcard or media clipping of interest to your target. Even if they said no, not interested, or voiced any other objection, for 50 cents and a few minutes of your time, it is a worthwhile investment.

Are you a packhorse?

Are you a packhorse? Do you carry around reports, spreadsheets, details and notebooks when you don't need to? I have seen managers and business owners going home on any given evening and virtually emptying their 'in tray' into their briefcase and taking it home only to carry it back into the office the next day virtually untouched! I know I have done it and on occasion I too can find myself stuffing more and more 'work' into my briefcase. But then I ask myself, is any of this actually going to get done tonight or am I just kidding myself?

City buses are full of executives with laptops and print outs trying to get another 30 minutes out of their workday! I would encourage you to leave all that material in the office and get better at managing your time and effectiveness when you are there. Use your time travelling or commuting to read or listen to CDs, MP3s or tapes on techniques that will improve your effectiveness. Manage and value your personal time as effectively as your professional time.

Air mail

I know that many of you regularly conduct mail outs to your prospect database. Here is a tip, which although small, can make a huge difference to your success rate. What is your first objective in any mail campaign? It is not the letter or the offer or the call to action, it is simply to get the prospect curious and interested in opening the envelope.

Today your prospects are used to being bombarded with offers, promotions, exclusive deals and 'once only' opportunities. When they first see your envelope, you have about 2 seconds before they have formed an opinion.

Here are two ways that will impact your response rate. Personalize your letter. There should be no letters addressed to 'The Manager' or 'Director', or worse still, 'Friend', 'Colleague' or 'Associate'.

Secondly, go to the Post Office and grab a few dozen free 'Air Mail' stickers and fix them onto a sample of your mail out. I can guarantee that the envelopes with the sticker and personalized name have a much greater chance of being opened than the others.

B.I.Y.E.R.S

I wrote earlier about the importance of leveraging your lists *(see page 75)*. I have also covered the four key 'personality' types of buyers you need to recognize when selling *(see page 48)*. I want to add to that knowledge with another system I have for quickly sorting out the hot prospects from the rubbish. This is essential when you are prospecting from a list or database unknown to you.

If you think about traditional prospecting (gold, diamonds, etc) what is the #1 product produced? It is **dirt, rocks, soil and sand**! 98% of what you will encounter is waste but to strike gold, you have to sort through the rubbish.

The key skill (apart from digging!) that a good prospector needs is an ability to tell the difference between gold and dirt.

It is the same in prospecting for sales and new business. A substantial number of your contacts on your lead list will be 'duds'. Let me introduce you to the model I use to grade or qualify prospects. I use the acronym '**B.I.Y.E.R.S**' this is both easy to remember and a valuable resource when I am working through a call list.

B = Begin NOW.

These are the scarcest and therefore the most valuable contacts on your list. They are ready to proceed now and are almost 'waiting' for you to call. The key thing is to identify them early. Many sales teams lose sales they never knew they had because they just happened to be at the end of their call list.

I = Interested at a specific date

These prospects are very interested in your product or service but at a specific time. Be careful that you are not being 'duped' and that they are genuinely interested. They then can be diarised for follow up.

Remember to always follow up with a service call much earlier than you agreed. Do not leave it to the time the prospect suggested.

Y = Yes - but

Yes, they are interested, but you cannot tie them down to a specific date, event or occasion. Follow up with a call shortly and either promote or demote them to I or E.

E = Envelopes

I call this group the 'Envelopes' because their request is for information. You know the response; can you send me a proposal, brochure, letter, details, quote etc. This group can be very dangerous because it is so easy for a good sales rep to be busy sending out information to what he considers 'hot prospects' when in reality the prospect is using this as a device to get rid of you.

Before you send anything out, make sure you have graded them correctly and you have a planned follow up.

R = Recycle and Recall

For whatever reason, maybe no contact, voice mail or gatekeepers etc, this contact did not move in either a positive or negative way. They should be kept on your database for future contact recycling, but NOT until you have completed the original list.

S = Suck

Finally there are those contacts who can suck the energy, focus, drive and motivation right out of your soul. These are people who are happy to give you a hard time. When you encounter one of these thank them politely, DELETE them from your list, hang up and move on to the next call ASAP. Rude people are in the minority but you don't have to deal with them. There are enough prospects in the market for you to prosper.

Bargain - I don't think so

When is a bargain not a bargain? Well, probably, most of the time. Let me explain. I have a very nice, new suit hanging up in my wardrobe. The only problem is that it does not fit me. The embarrassing thing is that it has never fitted me. Even when I bought it a year ago I knew that it did not fit me! So why would I part with money (which I am very fond of) for a product which I cannot use?

When I saw the suit, it was on sale and was hanging on a rack of other suits in various styles and sizes. As I sorted through the rack I already emotionally 'owned' the suit, all I had to do was find my size. But, you guessed it, my size was gone and this was the only one left.

What happened next was that my 'rational' brain started to sell me the idea that I could exercise and lose weight and that this was actually a good incentive for me to lose some weight. Well, I bought it and the suit is still hanging up unworn. The real lesson here is that what can first appear as a 'bargain' is in reality an expensive mistake and even when logic tells us so, our wants can override our needs.

When you have a client who is comparing your price with a 'cheaper' alternative, it is your responsibility as a professional to make certain that they are aware of the differences between price and value. I only wish that I had met a suit salesman that day and that he had given me similar advice.

Decision acceleration management

As sales professionals our market success is measured by the speed it takes our prospects to move from initial awareness to enthusiastic supporter. Our role and responsibility therefore is to understand the existing decision-making processes both rational and emotional for that executive or organization. To reduce the gaps, remove bottlenecks and speed up the process.

For our prospects, choosing a product or service is not a single decision, it is a series of decisions some of which are easier than others. Often our prospects are not aware themselves of their own decision making process. I use a process which I call the 'Wheel of Fortune', which separates the various stages of the decision making cycle. I encourage you to do the same.

There are several specific stages in the decision making process;

Contentment; "I don't have a problem"
Awareness; "I do have a problem"
Analysis; "What is the specific problem?"
Definition; "What are our resources?"
Selection; "Who can help me?"
Measurement. "What is the result?"

I recommend that you examine each of these stages and for all your 'pending' sales, identify at what stage they are, and develop tactics to help your prospect move forward through each stage.

Remember this?

In sales it can be a real asset to be able to remember prices and product details easily.

Most people do not believe they have a very good memory. In fact, they are convinced that they have a very poor memory. This is for the most part, untrue.

Here is a simple and effective way to prove to yourself that you can remember a random list of 10 objects. Let's start with a list you already know: Foot, Shin, Knee, Thigh, Stomach, Chest, Neck, Head, Eyes and Hair. The key to this list is that it starts at the bottom and works upwards. If you wanted it to be longer you could introduce more detail.

Next, list the items you want to remember, lets say groceries; Eggs, cheese, milk, bread, butter etc. This technique is called absurd association. When you want to recall the list, remember your foot standing on some eggs, then your shin turning into cheese, your knees are like lumps of bread, and someone has spread butter on your thighs.

The more you use your imagination to create images like this the easier it will be to remember any list with ease. Use your 'body list' and try it yourself, I think you will be surprised.

REFERRALS

We all know how valuable referrals can be to the success or failure of a sales campaign. A customer who is happy to be quoted or to tell their colleagues what a great job you have done can be your best representative in the marketplace.

The 'Rule of 16', well known in retail and service based industries, states that for every 'bad' job you do, one unsatisfied customer will tell 16 of their friends, colleagues and workmates. On the opposite side, for every delighted customer you have they will only refer you (when unprompted) once in every sixteen opportunities!

I am leaving it up to you to have a quality product or service in the marketplace that delights and satisfies your prospects. Frankly, if you have unhappy customers, attend to them NOW and stop the rot.

So what can we do to help those delighted clients refer business, both within their organization and externally, without putting pressure on them or harming the relationship? Many books I have read suggest getting **THEM** to call colleagues from **THEIR** desk while you are there. The reality is, most sales professionals feel uncomfortable when their colleagues and managers listen in, so how do you think your client is going to feel? There are easier and more effective ways to make this work.

When you ask the question,

> "Who else in your company has a similar problem that might also benefit from our service?"

The client may not be able to think of a name or names at that precise time and you are left with an 'awkward' silence. A way to remedy this is for YOU to suggest some names.

For example,

> "Mr Customer, I've identified four people in your company who I think would be the most likely users of our product, do you recognize any of these names?"

At that point HAND them over a printed list and let them study it. Only have a few names on the list and make sure they are at a similar level of seniority or lower than your customer. If they don't know any names on the list, I can almost guarantee they will suggest some new ones. You can then ask if they would mind if you contacted them.

Timing is all important. The ideal time to ask for referrals is just after they have bought your product and they have thanked you or made a positive comment about what you have done. If you lose the 'moment' and pick up the phone to ask at a later date, your chances of a positive response have diminished substantially.

Also ask in the right way. If you are not certain that your client is delighted with what you have done, DO NOT ASK! If they have to refuse, the embarrassment for both you and them will be immense and they will not be overly keen to speak to you again. As the saying goes,

> 'You will have snatched defeat from the jaws of victory.'

There is an easy way to set up your request for a testimonial. After the client has bought from you, but not yet experienced your offering, try this.

Quick TIP: Make ten calls each day before ten am to prospects you have not spoken to before.

"Mr Prospect, we plan to do a great job, if you agree we have, and you are delighted with the results, would you be happy to write a short testimonial?"

Before I begin…..

Once you have made an appointment, are in front of your prospect and have dispensed with the essential introductory small talk and personal introductions, an easy way to begin your 'sales' process is to tell them that you haven't begun yet! The last thing in the world you want a 'warmed up' prospect to notice is that the 'nice guy' is gone and you are now the 'sales rep' bearing down on their prey!

I use this technique on a daily basis,

"Before I begin, would you mind just walking me through…"

Using this with a nice expansive question allows your prospect to remain relaxed and for you to start examining their needs in more detail. Of course, when I say the words "before I begin", I have actually begun! This also works when you sense that a prospect is becoming more hesitant or reluctant to move forward. You could say,

"Before I go, there is just one thing I would like to ask."

Sometimes this is known as the 'Columbo' close made famous by Peter Falk in the 1970's American detective series of the same name. This question allows your prospect to lower their barriers because they believe you are about to go. Indeed you may be, but you never know where one little question could take you, do you?

Have you got $50,000?

Professionals in the investment community who sell their expertise and advice directly to the public (ie retail) have to be good at asking early qualifying questions. There are just too many people in the marketplace for them to waste their time talking to people who are just 'interested'.

They are looking for three things:

1. **Interest;** are they interested in your product or service?
2. **Authority:** Do they have the authority to make a decision?
3. **Money;** Do they have access to the minimum funds / budget necessary?

A question that works very well in this context is;

> "Mr Prospect, would you have $50,000 (or whatever your 'entry' price is) to invest if the opportunity was exactly what you were looking for?"

Now that is a pretty tough question and as you can imagine would generate a lot of 'No' answers. But in this environment that is exactly what is required because as soon as you get a yes, you know you have something to work with.

Can you hold?

What do you do when your phone rings? You pick it up of course and greet the caller. What if the caller says;

"Yes, it's John Doe here, I'm returning your call."

You have no idea who John Doe is and what you were calling him to pitch! You know you wanted to introduce something that was relevant to him, but it does not create a good first impression to 'emm' and 'ahh' and generally appear amateurish.

I suggest you do the following. If there is a good chance that their details are on your database, ask them to hold briefly and pull up their details. If you do not have immediate access to their details, explain that you have someone on the other line, and ask for their number so you can call them back in a few moments.

Most people will gladly give you their number. Then when you have gathered your thoughts / intelligence, you can call back and be in control and more confident.

Reciprocal concession – 'Trumped'

☑ Did you watch any episodes of the TV show 'The Apprentice'? Donald Trump may be one of the richest men in the world, but when it comes to interior design and hairdressing, he is distinctly challenged!

The show is produced by the 'Survivor' team. There are around sixteen contestants and each week, for one reason or another a member is eliminated until one is left and they become 'The Apprentice' and work for Trump.

You may recall that in the first episode, the contestants were broken into two teams (male and female) and given $250.00 to make lemonade and sell it on the street to passers-by. The team with the most amount of money at the end of the day would win. A fairly simple task.

What quickly became apparent was that everybody started 'doing' or selling **ASAP**. Not much effort went into strategy or planning how they were going to PERSUADE and convince strangers to pay $$$ for an open cup of lemonade from someone in a suit.

The dominant strategy employed was simply to stop people in the street and ask them if they would like to buy some lemonade. When the still walking target said NO they would then discount running along side them. They would then move on to the next stranger with the same tactic. If you want to experience this type of selling, just take a walk through most city centers.

Most of the team members were not salespeople. They were 'business' people. If you had been a member of that team, what could you have done to improve their success rate? I imagine the team would have welcomed you as a professional sales person, as one who earns their income directly from persuading and convincing others to buy, you would be perceived as an asset!

A technique which would have probably worked well would have been the use of **'Reciprocal Concession'**.

Here's how it works: You first make a large request. When your prospect declines your offer, you 'accept' their rejection and respond with a secondary 'lesser' request. In a lot of cases your second offer will be accepted.

Here is the reason WHY this works. The initial rejection from the prospect is seen by them as making YOU an 'offer' which they would like you to accept. When you concede to this, a part of them believes that you have done THEM a favor. Therefore, when you make a smaller secondary request they want to reciprocate and also make a concession.

Here is a short example:

>**Sales Person:** "Excuse me sir, would you like to take back a jug of lemonade for your colleagues in the office, only $15.00 and the money is for a good cause?"
>
>**Prospect:** "No thanks"
>
>**Sales Person** "Ok, but if you can't do that would you help by buying just one cup for only two dollars?

It has been proven by social scientists that this strategy works. In the case of our lemonade salesmen, they would have enjoyed substantially increased revenues had they stopped and prepared some techniques before they just 'jumped in'.

Reticular?

When something is bothering you, or you are considering a major purchase, investment or change do you begin to 'notice' more than usual that activity / or product around you? I'm sure most of you have had this experience but you have probably never been 'formally introduced' to it. I think it's about time you were. Welcome to your 'Reticular Activating System' (RAS).

It sounds complex, but is really rather simple. Consider the sheer amount of sensory information around us at any one moment in time; sight, sound, touch, smell, taste. If we focused on all of this content we could not cope, so our unconscious mind learns to 'filter' out what is not important.

When we consciously begin to think and consider something of importance, our unconscious mind makes a note. When it notices something related, it brings it to our attention. So it is only after you have bought that tie or coat which caught your eye that you begin to notice that everyone else is wearing one!

In a lot of first meetings our prospect's RAS is generally tuned in to their 'fears', those gestures or comments which we make which in turn can make them feel as if they are being sold to.

A lot of prospects over compensate this by being overly aggressive and trying to 'control' the conversation. In a sales interview, if you have such a prospect, it is a signal that you have not built rapport and trust and need to do so before moving forward in the sales process.

No forever?

Once they have received a 'NO' response and have moved on to other prospects on their database, many sales people NEVER call the original prospect back. Working on this basis, with a finite market, you are eventually going to run out of people to call, and those who do speak to you will put so much discount pressure on you, your life will be miserable.

There are two things I recommend. First, if you have exhausted your objection handling and still have a 'NO,' ask the prospect;

"Is that no for now or no forever?"

Most of the time it will be for now. So, ask them when you should contact them again, half that time period and diarise the follow up call. Make sure you have some evidence to deal with their core objection when you next call.

VIP Presenting

If you are ever presenting to a large group (10 plus) a good way to break the ice and start your presentation is to ask a generic question that you know will generate a 'yes' response.

Here's an example. Let's say you are a sales rep for a fashion label and are presenting a new range to a group of buyers from a major retailer. Rather than parade a list of features and benefits, ask the group a topic question you know they are interested in;

> "Before I begin... who here would really like to know the secrets to keeping floor stock moving without discounting and hurting yield?"

A show of hands will give you an idea of audience interest. Sometimes if I am speaking at a conference or very large function, I will keep 4 or 5 seats at the front marked as 'reserved' and ask a similar question. I will then offer these 'VIP' seats to audience respondents, give them a free gift such as a book or CD. Now you KNOW who is really interested and you know WHERE they are, so you can really deliver the presentation to them!

Kick in the 'Buts'

If you've ever heard yourself through tape recordings or role-plays you know it can be an uncomfortable experience. I believe listening to your own conversational style and voice patterns is probably the easiest way to improve your sales performance. When you do listen to these recordings the naked truth is revealed. This is what your clients hear.

One word which has crept into our language without us hearing it or being aware of how much we use it is the word 'but'. It has the power to greatly influence the impression your prospect has of your offering. Some examples I have heard sales people make include:

> "But if you look at it this way, but if you consider, but let me tell you, but many of your competitors, but it will only take" and so on.

Our prospects also use this word. Listen to this example;

> "John, thanks for all the effort you put in, **but** we have decided to go with ABC systems". Or; "Your solution certainly sounds impressive, **but** we are not in a position to buy at the moment".

Using the word 'but' in a sentence negates everything that came before it. The words prior to the 'but' are used simply to soften the hard end of the sentence that follows. You can't change what your prospects say, however you can listen and when you hear them using 'but' I can guarantee there is an objection about to be presented.

THE WORLD'S BEST SALES TIPS

As your greatest sales tool YOU have to be responsible for your own language and words. Try and get into the habit of replacing 'but' with 'and'. For example;

> "Mr prospect you mentioned you had a budget of only $25,000 *and* let me tell you why going over that is going to benefit your company."

By replacing the axis of the statement with 'and', it shows my prospect that I am listening and NOT disregarding their concerns. This requires a bit of practice and if you make it your own it will take you one step closer to being the professional you know you are.

How much is that puppy in the window?

☑ The 'Puppy Dog' close is one of the easiest and most powerful techniques in your sales arsenal. Pet stores know this and exploit it. Here is how it works; you and your 5 year old daughter are walking past a pet shop on a Friday and stop to look at all the cute puppies and kittens in the window.

You can see the delight on her face as she waves at them. Then you notice a sign in the window asking for 'volunteers' to take a puppy home for the weekend free of charge as the shop will be closed and they don't have the staff to look after them.

Hey, no risk, and you know that your daughter is going to be thrilled to bits. Everything is a roaring success, until something you may not have considered comes up. By Monday you are emotionally attached to 'Cuddles' (your daughter gave it a name) and it is unlikely that the puppy will make it back to the shop!

The pet shop and more sophisticated marketeers know this. Remember BMW letting you take home a brand new 3 Series for the weekend, **FREE**. It's really just a high ticket puppy. In the end Emotion ALWAYS wins over logic.

How much would you pay for a bucket of sand?

If I gave you a bucket of beach sand and told you that there was $20,000 worth of gold dust in it, what would you do? Would you start examining one grain of sand at a time, or would you say that it was too hard and the work required to sort the sand from the gold dust would cost more than the benefit? Perhaps you would employ other people to sort through it for you, but how could you be certain that they were being honest?

In the same way many sales people spend their sales careers working through the sand, grain by grain. It is hard work and the rewards are thin because of the TIME involved. In new business prospecting as well as gold prospecting you need to have a process that allows you to separate the sand from the gold simply and effectively.

For instance using water and a gold pan a prospector could get through that bucket in hours. As sales people our tools lie in our qualifying skills, database management and planning ability. Stop working the grains and start working the bucket!

Embedded commands

This major technique requires a little bit of brainwork however it is well worth the effort. An embedded command is a technique for placing a thought into the mind of your prospect without them perceiving that you are leading the conversation.

The technique is based on NLP (Neuro Linguistic Programming) principles and is delivered through the use of presuppositions, which are assumptions implied within spoken sentences. Think of an embedded command almost like a 'mental virus' used as a catalyst to get your prospect thinking in a particular way.

There are certain steps to using this persuasion technique. A lot of people will do these naturally in their day-to-day conversations and not be aware of them, but as sales people we can use them to be more persuasive and influential when presenting and negotiating. Here are the steps:

- Step 1: Wedge Phrase
- Step 2: Command Verb
- Step 3: States, Processes or Experiences you want them to imagine with Commanding Tonality

The first step is the Wedge phrase and acts as a suggestion to your prospect's mind. Wedge phrases are used to set up an embedded command. So phrases like; 'if you were to..', 'what would it be like..', 'imagine how...' etc.

The purpose of using embedded commands is to move our prospect's mind in the direction you want it to go without seeming to be intruding or ordering in any way. After the Wedge Phrase use a command verb, such as 'get', 'become', 'experience', 'remember', etc.

Then mention the state, process or experience you want your prospect to remember or imagine and you have created an embedded command.

In most western countries, spoken commands end with a down turn in tonality. Embedded commands mandate the use of a commanding tonality to be effective. Avoid an uplift in your tone at the end of a phrase as it can sound like a request to the prospect.

So in summary, together with a commanding tonality (you need to practice this) the three elements are:

Wedge phrases: if you were to..', 'what would it be like..', 'imagine how…'

Command verbs: become, think about, get, remember, experience, have…..

States: confident, happier, in control, successful, winning, relaxed etc

Use this structure to create your own commands that relate to your product or service. Here is a relevant example;

> "Imagine how you will be more confident when you start using this technique with prospects."

Proposal pointers

I have certain guidelines regarding written proposals that I would like to share with you.

Most importantly, I tend NOT to write proposals unless I know that I have either won, or if I am very likely to win the business. It is just too easy for clients to ask you to write a proposal when what they really want is to get rid of you or leverage your price.

Next, aim to keep your document to three A4 pages or less and use 'Bullet Points' as the main text. No long prose and waffle. Include appendices, research and testimonials in a separate pre-formatted document.

Almost **NEVER** send the proposal to your prospect prior to your presentation. If you cannot present (because of time / location etc) then you may have to send it, however make it a living document and include personal notation throughout *(also see page 70)*.

Finally, the document should be supplementary to your presentation. Leave it at the end. The proposal should not contain any surprises for the client. It should really only act as a confirmation of their needs and the value of your strategy.

Demonstrate before you 'presentate'

Whenever you are planning to present to a client or prospect, find a way to demonstrate your product's features and benefits. If you have a tangible product such as a copier or car this can seem really straightforward but you need to demonstrate the benefits as well as the features, that's a lot harder.

Too many presentations are dull and lifeless. They really could be so much more engaging if the 'demonstrate' rather than 'presentate' principle was applied. A simple way to affect this even when you are selling services is to use props as a metaphor for your service.

For instance, if you wanted to show that you had the 'key' to your prospect's success you could bring a physical door into the presentation, act out the frustration of trying to open it with the wrong keys and then the right key, your solution, opens it with ease.

Demonstrations rehearsed and delivered well are memorable. They have more impact and give you the edge you need when the client is deciding who to give their business to.

Do you know how to flash?

Have a look at the phone on your desk. It is the most important business tool that you have at your disposal, but how well do you know it? Do you know how to place calls on hold or transfer them? Do you have key numbers on speed dial to save time looking up numbers and punching in the keys?

I would guess that even though it is a fairly sophisticated piece of equipment and has a lot of bells and whistles you probably use your telephone like a basic handset.

I am realistic enough to realise that this book is not going to get you racing around looking for the manual or booking into a 'how to' phone training program, so here is one tip that you can use right NOW. Does your phone have a 'flash' button, most do. If it does, do you know what it is for?

The next time you are making outbound calls rather than hang up, just press the flash button and 'bingo bango' you will have a dialing tone. This is great when you are really 'humming' and want to increase your call rate.

Double marketshare anyone?

Imagine the following scenario, there are five companies in a new market category, all selling a similar product to a similar market. If their average sales cycle takes 12 months then at the end of their first year trading (same effort and skill) each company should have around 20% market share.

Now imagine a little bit more, you are the C.E.O. of company number one. After the first year of trading there is not much between any of the competitors. However at the start of year two you and your team discover, or create, a way to cut your internal, and your client's decision-making time, by 50%. What would the market look like at the end of year two?

Remember, you are not necessarily more talented in sales or business development. Your product is exactly the same as your competitors, and everyone is selling to the same customer base, all the companies have the same resources, cash and products. Your only advantage is in getting client's to make decisions in half the time of your competition.

Simple logic says that six months into your second year you will have 20% market share while your four competitors are struggling to understand why their sales are lagging. At the end of year 2, you will have a minimum of 40% share. Although the reality is that because of your strong position earlier in the year, word of mouth, and market leadership, this would most likely be around 70%. Your competitors are fighting amongst themselves for the remaining 30%.

How can this be, is it really that simple? No, it is a lot more complex and there are many other variables, but if you can reduce the TIME it takes for you, your team and your clients to make decisions then you will enjoy substantial growth at the expense of your competition.

To achieve this growth requires a change of attitude towards business development. It requires more 'upstream' than 'down stream marketing'. Upstream marketing is BEFORE the client / prospect has identified a need rather than 'ambulance chasing' after they have recognized a problem and are looking for a vendor.

Upstream marketing and consultative selling means you need to understand the prospect's problem and identify where the decision bottlenecks are. Your job is to remove them or find other, simpler, alternate routes around them.

I suggest you begin this process internally rather than externally. If you can force yourself to make decisions more quickly, even if they are WRONG, you will benefit. As you learn from your mistakes you will make fewer of them. Your selling, management speed and effectiveness will multiply.

Just say NO!

Sometimes the hardest thing to do as a sales person is to say 'no' to a deal. Have you ever had a client say 'yes' to your proposal or idea however there was that feeling in the pit of your stomach that something was not quite right?

Later this feeling is justified when the customer is unhappy or requires more 'hand holding' and servicing than the contract merits. Mark McCormack in 'Success Secrets' identifies three reasons to walk away from a sale:

1. When you can't deliver or exceed their expectations

2. When the price and one other ingredient don't add up. Sometimes it may be worth discounting to win a strategic piece of business but if there is no long-term value and it is a one off, perhaps you should walk away.

3. When they demand you abandon your principles. This is key to your brand and reputation and in reality you are 'future discounting' by accepting this type of work.

Sell to me in the kitchen

This tip is for sales professionals that sell 'retail' in their prospects' homes. Industries like insurance, alarm companies, architects, builders and many more.

Firstly make sure you have both partners present, even if one says they make the decision. Encourage their wife or husband / partner to be there, often they will hold the balance of power.

Secondly try to get the sales conversation / interview in the kitchen. Kitchens are generally brighter, have a larger table to place your paperwork, etc on and are associated with family decisions. This is where families discuss important decisions, so you should be there, too.

Thirdly when selling at home behave as if you were a guest and take your time. Allow for much longer appointment times and have the flexibility to extend if you need to.

Being in a prospect's home you should respect their space, be patient and be aware of their emotional issues.

Call me back – no, you call ME back

Here is a simple, productive tip that can free up your time and emotional energy.

You probably receive lots of calls and interruptions from internal staff and suppliers throughout the day. Most people in your situation will either stop what they are doing to attend or tell the person that they will call them back later.

Offering to call back puts the onus on you and if you forget, you will carry the blame. If they want to speak to you, you can use this as an advantage and manage your time better.

Try the following simple strategy. When someone interrupts your schedule, ask THEM to call you back at a time when you can deal with those types of issues. You should set aside time in your day for administration etc which is NOT your prime selling time. In this way, you do not need to worry about getting back to them, they will look after that for you and you can get back to what you do best, contacting your future clients.

Let them try before they buy

Selling your product is so much easier if you can make it personally relevant to your prospect by creating an immediate sense of ownership.

Here is an example of how this strategy can be used in Radio advertising sales.

John Doe our radio rep is spending a day cold calling door to door on local businesses with a standard,

> "I was just passing and wondered if you would be interested…"

He is in for a long and unprofitable day, doors slammed, no thanks, not interested, no money etc.

What if a day or two prior our sales rep had taken a 'generic' 15 second ad and spent a few hours taping a 'rough' commercial, using information in the yellow pages for ten prospects in his area. Then when making his 'cold' visits, he could have used a script like this,

> "Mr Prospect, my name is John Doe. I have helped hundreds of companies like yours get great results from radio. Rather than just tell you about it, the best way to prove this to you is to play you your own commercial. It's right here in my hand and I would love to play it for you now."

At this stage John has a hand held recorder with the trial commercial on it. Most business owners will want to hear it and most will then ask questions (buying signals). This type of strategy works, I used it for years with dummy layouts in print advertising.

Get on your front foot

I'm sure you are familiar with the expressions 'being on your back foot' or 'being on your front foot'. Generally they are used to describe someone who is either caught off balance or is being proactive and / or assertive.

However, there is more to this than a simple illustration. When you stand with the weight of your body either on your toes or your heels it can have an impact on how your message is delivered and received. When you present, your body language needs to be congruent with the language and tonality of your message.

In situations where you are nervous or need to demonstrate confidence you need to quite literally put your weight onto your front foot and keep it there. The other foot just touches the ground to maintain balance. This posture straightens the spine and will change your tone and perceived assertiveness. It sounds easy, however in my experience few people can maintain this position for longer than a couple of seconds without practice. Try it at your next presentation.

Kindy sales lessons

Children are the best sales people in the world. They NEVER take no for an answer. They are persistent to the point of lunacy, they take a 'maybe' or 'I'll think about it' as a definite YES, they remember when you don't and when it comes to negotiating they always focus on the emotional motivators rather than the rational!

If you are a sales manager, you can learn from children. Why do they display the skills and tenacity that you want in your team when they haven't read a sales book, been trained or read any 'sales tips' newsletters? And why does your team seem to be missing these fundamentals?

The key is the children are PERSONALLY motivated. As a sales manager you will get a LOT more performance for your salaried dollar from your sales team if you can relate their activity to how it will impact on their lives in a positive way. Use the **PREPARE** model *(see page 29)* to really hone in on their emotional drivers.

Lead, follow or get out of the way

You know it is not possible for you to lead in everything that you do. Sometimes a better strategy is to follow and learn from the mistakes of others. If and when the timing is right, step up and take a leadership position or stay as #2. In fact often a followers position can be more profitable. Think of Avis car hire's positioning 'We Try Harder'

In 1962, just before the first 'We Try Harder' commercials launched, Avis was an unprofitable company with 11% of the car rental business in the USA. Within a year of launching the campaign, Avis was making a profit, and by 1966 Avis had tripled its market share to 35 percent! Before this, Hertz was the clear leader in the car rental business, with Avis as one of the brands in the following pack.

The Avis campaign re-positioned Hertz creating a relative, believable and compelling brand for Avis. The market dominance of Hertz became a weakness and Avis became the 'right choice' in the mind of consumers.

If your product or service is not the market leader, you can adapt this strategy to fit into your sales presentations to great effect. If you are #1 you can also use it. Rupert Murdoch was asked once how his businesses managed to stay at the #1 spot and he replied "..by always acting like we are #2."

"As our new sales manager there are plenty of opportunities for growth!"

Sometimes it pays to be inconsistent

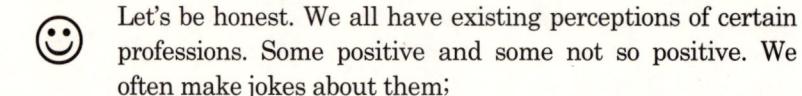

Let's be honest. We all have existing perceptions of certain professions. Some positive and some not so positive. We often make jokes about them;

'How do you recognize an extrovert accountant? Well, they look at YOUR shoes when they are talking to you!'

(My apologies to any sensitive number crunchers out there). There is no shortage of jokes about lawyers, doctors, politicians and of course sales people!

What makes each joke funny is that there is usually a grain of truth at the center. This grain of truth is an insight into your prospect's perceptions of your chosen career.

Most people are familiar with the cliché of the second hand car salesman and much as we like to think our prospects don't regard us in that way, until we prove differently, that is how most people in 'sales' are considered.

As sales professionals we need to demonstrate to our prospects that we are NOT consistent with this image. We need to get them to reconsider us as individuals who are not the norm, and as such, it PAYS to look for opportunities to behave inconsistently with their negative perceptions.

Sales can be broken down into many categories; Insurance, Real Estate, Financial Services, Retail, Broking etc and for each one there is a slightly different predisposition within your target market. I would encourage you to do two things when you have finished reading this page.

1. Conduct a straw poll amongst colleagues and customers and ask them what were or are their perceptions?

2. Gather the information, anecdotal or otherwise and compile a table.

You can then use this to brainstorm ways to demonstrate to your prospects that you are NOT like all the others. Then build these strategies into your daily prospecting and business development activities. Understand what your prospects expectations are and CONSISTENTLY go further.

All the top performers in any field have a growing number of clients who act as their marketing 'legs'. They are delighted to refer colleagues through to you because they know their associates will be as delighted with your service as they were. Before you get to this point you have to be ready to challenge your own perceptions and predispositions first.

Story selling

The best sales people in the world are great storytellers. If you were to listen to them 'selling' there would be no obvious technique or hidden secret. They would relate various situations, often humorous, to something that happened to them and illustrate how their service or product helped someone else in a similar situation.

Sales professionals and customers alike communicate to others through stories. There is a beginning, middle and an end and there is a reason or moral to the story. When starting out in sales or in a new sales role it is easy to focus on product knowledge alone. This knowledge is critical, but find a way to relate it to something you have done or experienced which will be much more engaging for your prospect.

Working longer and harder

For this and previous generations there has long been the philosophy that if you work hard and 'put in the hours' then eventually you will succeed. This is NOT true and it is a difficult habit to change, especially if you run your own business or work for yourself.

Remember that the terms 'hard' and 'long' are subjective, they mean different things to different people. What I consider hard or difficult someone else may find easy and straightforward, and vice versa. The problem with this is unless we are measuring our activity by results, we can fool ourselves into thinking that eventually the effort will be worth it.

If by changing work practices you could achieve the same result in five years rather than twenty, shouldn't you reconsider your 'effectiveness' paradigm?

The key is being effective in what you do and how you manage others. Jack Collis' book 'Work Smarter NOT Harder' deals with this subject in detail. I recommend it to you.

A real and present opportunity

Large numbers of sales people make the error of trying to sell to everyone who seems interested rather than someone who has a real and present need. Think about this scenario, a sales rep picks up an incoming call and starts dealing with an inquiry from a fact-finding shopper. Thinking he has a 'hot' prospect he tries every which way and eventually persuades the caller to agree to an appointment where he can present his full range.

The rep is keen to do this because he has a quota of field sales calls to make and although this is a bit out of his way, every call counts. Ask yourself; is this a good use of sales time, energy and resources? Almost certainly not. Worse still, the prospect may stay on the 'maybe' list for months, with lots of follow up calls and sales activity reports, but NO real sale.

The real sales champions detect and qualify who the REAL buyers are and manage / prioritize their time accordingly. Their technique and ability to engage etc can be exactly the same as ordinary performers, yet because they qualify EARLY they enjoy substantially larger sales success. Take a look at your next 'opportunity' is it real or is it just an opportunity for you to lose money?

No thanks we're happy

Earlier in the book I touched on what to say when you come across the objection; 'No thanks, we're happy with our current supplier' *(see page 44)*. I want to go into that in a bit more detail for several reasons;

1. The chances are that if your prospect has a recognized existing need for your type of product or service, then someone else is already supplying them and they are going to tell you thanks but no thanks etc.

2. Gatekeepers use this objection frequently to get rid of sales calls, even when they do not have an existing supplier.

3. Related to 2 above, most sales people accept this objection and just move on without getting some critical information.
4. If you can improve your strike rate when handling this objection, even by a small percentage, you will enjoy dramatically increased sales over the medium term.

Here's a typical initial sales call:

> **Prospect**: "Yes, John Prospect Speaking"
>
> **Salesperson**: "Hi John, thanks for taking my call, it's Peter Sells here from Acme Industries. The reason I wanted to speak with you today is that recently we have had a great deal of success with other companies in your sector who are using the XYZ 3000 to not only reduce their overall costs but at the same time improve their revenues by over 25%!"
>
> **Prospect**: "Ehhh, no thanks we are happy with our current supplier."

This is a typical first objection and one that I am sure most of you have heard many times before. Depending on how you have read their tone of voice you could respond with the **'That's Great'** strategy:

> **Salesperson**: "That's great, but before I go, would you mind telling me, what is it that they do so well?"

Prospects love responding to this because it reinforces their position and they believe it is helping to get rid of you. Most of them will then proceed to give you at least two or three

✓ **Quick TIP**: The easiest source of new prospects are you and your client's neighbors.

areas where they believe your competitors have an advantage. Make sure you are busy taking notes of all their points. When they are finished you then throw in the stinger:

> "and what do you think they could improve on?"

The beauty of this technique is that your prospect will most likely be happy to give you a list of areas where you will have the greatest opportunity to compete effectively. Resist the temptation to use this information in the moment, just capture their points, thank them and then when you call back in a week or so your opening statement can be built on this critical info. For example;

> "Mr prospect I was thinking about a number of the points you raised last week and I don't know if you are aware…"

Procrastination

Have you ever had a really busy day, but got nothing done of any significance? Do you look at your desk and the papers, files, folders, memos and the chaos and give up? Well you are not alone. The sales community is not exactly known around the world for their administrative skills, desk neatness, and having a sense of order and process.

It is all too easy when you work within a medium or larger sized sales team to 'hide' and accept the average performance and habits of the group even if when you joined, you had higher standards.

Everyone, then starts playing 'blame the company or manager for their problems. As a quick thumbnail in sales you should take your OTE (on target earnings) salary plus expenses, super and medicare and multiply that number by at least three. In different industries because of the cost of goods, manufacturing etc, this may vary. But if you are not bringing in three times your salary you need to get fired with enthusiasm or sooner or later you will be enthusiastically fired!

Are you a $400,000k sales professional?

Are you a $40,000 sales rep who is earning $40,000, or are you a $400,000 sales professional who is currently earning $40k? If you are behaving and acting like a $40k rep, then that is probably where you will stay.

If you can act, prospect and market yourself and your products / services as if you were a $400k professional then we both know that it is only a matter of time before your career moves into the space you deserve.

The cliché, 'your attitude determines your altitude' is so true. It is NEVER too late to change, even if you have been in the same role for 20 years and have essentially behaved in the same way. You can change your horizon if you wish. But you have to accept the personal, social and financial risk of initial failure and / or embarrassment.

You can greatly reduce the impact of this with a plan. Earlier in the book *(see page 64)* I mentioned 'If you haven't got a plan, you're a tourist!' Stop wandering around in your job and start your sales career, TODAY.

The 'R' word

A while back I spoke at an industry investment seminar on Australia's Gold Coast. Most of what was discussed and presented was not immediately relevant for us as consumers, but there were a few things that grabbed my attention.

Several people were talking about the 'R' word, Recession. Interest rates of 10%, a global oil crisis, slowing domestic economy and overextended mortgages all contributing to a tougher selling environment, hey bring on the optimists!

Just imagine for a moment that I had been able to leap a couple of years into the future and come back and report that this IS going to happen. What would you do about it right NOW?

Perhaps you would get more organized, improve on the key skills you would need to sell in this environment. Try and earn as much as you can now rather than later, and invest. My question is why would you not do these things now anyway, regardless of the future markets. If they make good sense now, get busy now.

More 'RUST'

Several times in this book I have focused on standard ways of handling objections from your initial sales call to a cold prospect. The first couple of objections are not objections to the sales per se, but are rather objections to actually taking the call from you and having a discussion.

The prospect is not consciously lying to you, they are just busy people, you have interrupted them, they have no idea who you are and let's face it most of the calls they receive are a waste of their time.

A few years ago I was working with a new sales team who were being hammered with first objections from gatekeepers. Typically, the standard; "We're not interested, we've no time, sorry no money or no need!" Their activity was good and I knew they had the sales ability.

I just needed a simple way for them to remember how to handle those first objections and I knew their sales would soar. The key was getting to the third or fourth objection, because that is usually the real one.

Earlier in the book I touched on the 'RUST' technique *(see page 70)* which handles the initial objection and takes you to the next objection. Let's look the technique again in a little more detail. Here is a typical scenario:

> **Sales Pro**: "Good morning, is that XYZ Supplies? (yes), Great it's John Sells here (pause) who am I speaking to?"
>
> **Gatekeeper**: "Jane Lockes."
>
> **Sales Pro**: "Jane, I was wondering if you could help me, do you know who looks after purchasing in your company?"

At this point you may either get a contact name or what is more likely the next response:

> **Gatekeeper**: "What's it in regard to?"

Sales Pro: *at this stage use your planned opening statement (see page 1). You are still likely to get a no response.*

> **Gatekeeper**: "Sorry we're not interested" (said with a matter of fact tone!)

Now make sure your response is said with a little humour in your vocal tone. It's easy to do, just smile while you say it:

> **Sales Pro**: "Jane, aRe yoU just Saying That to get me of the phone?"

Nine times out of ten they are surprised by your response and will answer YES also with a little humour in their voice. At this stage **YOU SHUT UP.**

They will then give you your second objection. It does not really matter what it is because you know how to handle all of them right?

If you are in the sales business, dealing with this is your bread and butter.

Sales Housework

If you are like me, you hate housework. Dusting, vacuuming, window cleaning, laundry and more and then more! There are three ways to manage it:

1. A little work, on a regular basis,
2. A lot of work less frequently or
3. Pay some one else to do it.

The most effective is #1. A little bit, a lot of the time. Sales administration (self management) is the same.

The end of a quarter, month, financial or calendar year is a great opportunity for you to review practices and behaviors which need a little housekeeping. How is your prospecting activity? Have you set aside a part of each day for new business calls? What is your most profitable product and who are your most loyal customers? What customers do you want next period and how many?

Many of you have a sales manager and administrative staff in your team, but YOU need to run this side of YOUR business. Remember; budget your activity first before you budget dollars and constantly calibrate and measure your performance. A little work on a regular basis goes a long way *(see page 39)*.

The last minute...

☑ When you are working on a competitive proposal or pitch be aware of the 'recency' effect. This means that the closer your offer is to your prospect's deadline the more powerful it can be.

It is obvious that if yours is the first proposal or the only proposal, your prospect has the time to 'shop around'. They can use your price as a benchmark from which to measure others. If your proposal was in early or you become aware that the prospect is price shopping then you can be assured they WILL find a cheaper alternative. The best option in my opinion is to be last.

Dollar driven car dealers will use this tactic. When dealing with tire kickers they will say,

> "Shop around, get your best price, and come to us last and we will beat it!"

But when a prospect *is* talking to you last and you don't like discounting (and I hate it) you need to keep something in reserve which you can use in the final stages to add value and push your offer over the line.

If you have done your homework and questioned effectively *(see page 29),* time your offer to your greatest advantage, so they are closer to the deadline and you have the greatest leverage.

Right NOW!

I have a large clock that hangs on my office wall. Most office walls have clocks on them, nothing unusual about that. But in the center of my clock is a large printed sticker that I put there to remind me of my most precious resource: TIME!

The sticker says: "What is the best use of your time RIGHT NOW?" Every time I glance at it, it reminds me to be constantly re-evaluating my current activity in line with my sales outcomes.

This little sticker has helped me make many thousands of dollars by getting me to stop worthless activities and pick up the phone one more time.

Networking - notworking

A client recently invited me to one of their product launch functions. Plenty of food, wine, guests, brochures, speeches and small talk.

Typically, when a corporate function like this is scheduled the sales team is asked to create a list of the clients whom they would like to attend. The list is submitted then culled and invitations wing their way into offices across the country.

Thousands of dollars are spent hiring rooms, coaching speakers, printing brochures, press releases and kits and many hours committed to organising, managing and facilitating the event. But WHY?

Why do large and small businesses go to this trouble and stress on a regular basis? What is alarming are the vague responses you will get if you ask this question in your own company.

> "To tell people about our new widget....so that everyone knows about it...because it is better than the competition....."

The only reason is to create an interest in and eventually sell the product or service. The sales cycle may be longer but at the end of the day the business wants to generate profitable sales.

With that objective in mind what do you find most sales people doing at these types of functions? At most client launches / releases it would be the exception for a guest to be approached by ANY person from within the company. Most sales people can be found in groups of three or four fellow sales people enjoying their employer's hospitality with a few drinks and nibbles. Most of them will only speak to a couple of their best accounts and that's on a good day. What a waste!

If you are planning an event you need to have created and communicated a networking plan. Your sales team need to have clear performance outcomes; numbers of new contacts approached, key clients engaged, referral introductions made. They need to know how to demonstrate the product and its benefits. Observe their movements and break up internal gatherings that are going on for too long.

These events are excellent opportunities to build rapport with prospects and create leads for lasting future relationships. Make sure they are not wasted.

What's the difference?

What would your response be to a prospect who says they don't perceive any difference between your product and your competition? Straight away this sort of comment tells me that you have not done a good enough job understanding their priorities and critical issues. Product and prospect knowledge is key and as a professional you need to know both yours and your competitors inside out.

Find something that your prospect is passionate about (like a football team) and then create an analogy saying something like,

> "Mr Prospect, when you look at most teams at the top of the league there is not much to separate them,…. often just the small details, perhaps one or two players will determine whether they get a medal or not. It is the same with us, let me tell you about the critical differences which will ensure that your decision is with the winning team…."

The magic moment...

☑ When does a 'sale' happen? Is it the moment a cheque is handed over, or is it the moment a prospect says the word 'Yes'. Opinions vary, but my favorite definition is, the second the 'light bulb' goes on above your prospect's head and they realize that it will cost them MORE if they do nothing about the problem or issue rather than take action and follow your advice. So how do you recognize the moment? It would be great if all our prospects actually had real light bulbs over their heads and when they 'got it' we could see the light coming on.

My suggestion is this; imagine that this light bulb over their head has a dimmer knob, rather than an on/off rocker switch. Each question that the client asks is an opportunity for you to and turn the knob slightly. You may need to do this only once, six or twenty times, but each time the intensity of your case will grow stronger and finally your prospect will see the light!

Get a handle on the outcome

☑ One of my clients recently passed on this short but great tip and I thought I would share it with you.

If you have ever played golf you may recall that a key strategy before you play your stroke is to visualize the backswing, downswing, the club face hitting the ball perfectly with the sweetspot sound before the ball is flying its way towards the pin. Once your goal has been visualized it is a long way toward being realized.

When walking into a sales situation my client suggested that when placing your hand on the door to the company's office, boardroom or suite you visualize yourself LEAVING with a successful sale under your belt! This is a great way to set yourself up for success. As soon as your hand touches a door or you walk into a lobby, use the experience in the moment to create a clear image in your mind's eye of you grinning on your way out having achieved your objective!

Optimism

There is one book that all sales managers and sales people should read: 'Learned Optimism' by Seligman. Although you may think you can, you cannot tell by gut feel alone whether you are an optimist or a pessimist. In Seligman's remarkable book he has a self-scoring test comprising of some 48 questions, which will give you a rating and confirm where you really are.

Why is this important? Well if you are in the sales business you are going to get a lot of rejection and how you deal with that rejection will be just about the # 1 reason behind your success or failure in sales and many other aspects of your life. You don't have to be an optimist to succeed. I was surprised when my test results indicated that I am a mild pessimist!

The important issue is HOW you deal with rejection once you know what your preference is. This moves into the area of self-talk and internal dialogue. That little voice inside your head which gives you praise comment or critique, sometimes just when you don't need it!

Seligman's research uncovered that when bad things happen to pessimists, such as a rude customer response from a cold call, they tend to internalize their self dialogue and 'talk' using language that is Personal, Pervasive and Permanent.

Look at this typical example of negative self talk by a sales person after being rejected:

"I'll never be any good at this".

Let's break it down and look at each element in turn:

'I'll' – It is my fault, it's personal
'never' – it's permanent
'at this' – it's pervasive or non specific

Whereas optimists tend to do the opposite. A typical self dialogue for an optimist might be;

"He was in a bad mood when I called".

This language is External, Specific and Temporary.

'He was' – It is their fault, it's external
'in a bad mood' – there was a specific reason why
'when I called' – it's temporary

It is not better or worse to be one or the other, however there are some real dangers in being either extremely optimistic or extremely pessimistic. If I am hopping onto a 747 to London, I don't want an extreme optimist as a pilot. If anything I want someone who is slightly pessimistic and will double-check everything.

As sales professionals our #1 task is managing ourselves and that means controlling the messages we send ourselves when things get tough.

The next time you make a call and get rejected, challenge your internal dialogue and make it external, specific and temporary. And if you are managing others look for all the nuances in their everyday language. You can quickly tell what a person's preference may be.

And introducing...

When presenting to a large group in a theatre, boardroom or conference room and an 'emcee' is introducing you, there are two essential things you must do to make you and your audience feel a lot more confident and build anticipation for your presentation.

Firstly, make sure that YOU write your introduction and give it to the 'emcee'. They may change and adjust it, but both of you will be the better for it. By the way, strike a balance between being fairly modest and blowing your own trumpet.

Secondly, if you can, begin your presentation as soon as you start to walk towards the lectern. Do not walk up in silence and rearrange papers and notes or have a quick cough before you begin, it is too much like a sermon or eulogy. Just craft an interesting observation that you can make on your way up. Watch the professionals, they all do this.

Your staff are your customers

If you are a sales manager I encourage you to stop thinking of your team as employees and start regarding them as your customers. THEIR customers are their focus. Imagine if the individuals on your team were actually your customers, what sort of information would you want to gather? How would you communicate and how would you influence, persuade and motivate them?

Just like real customers some of them will require more work and effort and some will need little encouragement. The critical thing is that by changing your attitude towards them they will be empowered and motivated to drive your business successes!

Chimney referrals

Every sales person loves referral leads. A client, colleague or associate gives you a name and contact details and a reason to call. Perhaps they have even spoken to the prospect and they have asked for you to call them! Certainly this type of a sales lead would fall into the 'hot' prospect category.

Here is a way that can help create the same referral impression when you are calling into large organizations. I call it creating chimney referrals. The strategy is about gaining entry through the top of the business rather than the cellar entry.

Both types of entry can be hard work but the cellar strategy will generally have cold responses from gatekeepers and dim levels of enthusiasm from switchboard operators. The chimney although hotter and with a greater potential to get 'burned' will take you straight into where your decision makers live.

Lets say that you have been calling CIO's (Chief Information Officers) of large firms in your area with little or no success. 99% of the time you are being stonewalled by PA's and receptionists who have been told not to let ANY sales people through. You have tried everything, but your strike rate is pretty poor and you don't hold out much hope for the rest of the so-called 'Gold' prospecting list your sales manager gave you.

Do this; make your first call to someone higher in the organization, in this case the CEO or Chairman. The chances of you getting through to that person are pretty remote. Most of the time, you've guessed it, you will reach their PA, secretary or assistant.

But this time don't sell, ASK. Of course use a good opening statement and explain who you and your company are, but ask them who looks after that area in the business. In this instance they will give you the name of the CIO, you may already have that, but that is not the important point.

After thanking them you can make another call to the CIO's office and when the gatekeeper asks;

> "What is your call in reference to?" or "Does he know you?" or the classic; "Will he know what the call is regarding?"

> You can answer quite truthfully; "I was referred to him from John Doe's office (where John Doe is the name of the CEO)."

✓ **Quick TIP**: Get immediate improvement in call quality by recording your calls.

Your chances of getting through have just multiplied or at the very least if you have to leave a message, they will call you back.

When you are connected through to your prospect, make sure that a part of your introduction clarifies the fact that you were speaking to the PA. Sometimes this strategy works out even better because in your first call the CEO's PA will actually transfer your call directly to the prospect's office.

Is that the best you can do?

☑ The best way to learn how to negotiate is when **YOU** are buying not selling. After all, you probably buy items and services a lot more frequently than you sell. So the next time you are faced with a sales person offering a price, reply with either the initial flinch *(see page 8)* and ask them:

> "Is that the best you can do?"

Then be quiet, not a sound! You will be surprised how many sales staff will offer you a discount. When you are dealing with a competent sales person their reply should be along these lines:

> "That's the best price we have on this model at this quantity, but if you can do without (feature / benefit of product) we do have another which is cheaper."

The great thing about this reply is that the sales executive is saying yes there is a better price, but you need to lift your total spend. If they have qualified and engaged you well enough they also know that the feature they just suggested removing is one of the key reasons driving your purchase.

Take every opportunity you can get to negotiate, and benefit both from increasing your ability and getting discounts that no one else can.

Paperwork panic

If your sales activity and closing requires your client to sign a contract to formalize their commitment, then like a lot of sales people you probably hate that 'moment' when you pull out a large serious legal looking form. The prospect suddenly has a look of fear!

"Oh Oh, I'm being sold something!"

You do not want to lose the sale at this point. Here are a number of tips that will make this less of an obstacle.

If you are in their office or home, either start the sale with the document in view of everyone. Or, when it comes to taking it out, make sure you have other contracts, all filled in and signed. Take a few moments to find a blank one. This gives your prospect the sense that lots of others have committed and there is safety in numbers.

Should your prospect be in your office for the negotiation, then make sure your 'in' tray is piled high with completed contracts. You can even use this as a close by having an express courier bag marked up and indicating that all the orders in the tray have to be sent to head office tonight to get the special (bonus / value). Tomorrow is too late!

I want to think it over….

Oh dear, sounds like trouble. I'm guessing that you have heard that statement or one very similar to it quite a few times in your career. If you are not hearing it, you either have a monopoly and everyone has to buy from you or you are not prospecting enough!

We all know that the chances of your prospect actually thinking about it are remote and of course, when you call back they don't want to look foolish (because they haven't thought it over) so they 'bend' the truth a little and make the 'safe' decision. Unfortunately, this does not involve you and your wonderful widget or gizmo. In this tip I want to focus on a strategy for this objection when you are face to face with your prospect.

You have cold called, set up an appointment, perhaps written a proposal and even held a second meeting, so you have invested a lot of time and energy into this sale. Here is what I want you to do:

You will be using a number of techniques in combination. First **'That's Great'** *(page 112)*, then a version of **'RUST'** *(page 116)* and followed by the **'Columbo'** *(page 87)* technique.

The first thing you should do is look delighted and use this statement;

> "That's great!, I know you wouldn't do that unless you were going to give my proposal serious consideration, would you?"

This is important because they are not expecting you to be happy about this and it throws them off balance for a second or two, just enough time for them to hurriedly respond to your closed question (would you?) and say YES to the fact they are going to give it 'serious consideration'. They are hardly going to contradict themselves and say no, are they?

After they have responded, you should look as if you are happy with their response and then look them in the eye and use the **RUST** technique;

> "John, you're not just saying that to get rid of me are you?"

Again, the prospect will tend to respond by confirming their serious interest in your proposal.

That's when you can use the 'Columbo' close and say,

> "Well, before I go, would you mind telling me what it is that you want to think over, is it our (product / service specification)?"

The way the phrase is structured is critical to the success of this strategy. If you notice, the question is delivered in such a way as to elicit a 'No' response. It is really two questions joined at the hip with 'is it...' as the glue.

So for instance, our question could be,

> "Before I go, would you mind telling me what it is that you want to think over, is it our delivery specifications?"

Do not pause between the two statements. Prospects will tend to respond with denials, unless of course you are lucky enough to stumble on the real objection. So in this example their response would probably be along the lines of;

"No, no, its not your delivery specifications"

Now we are set because we can now gently ask a series of 'is it' type questions; is it our color range? Is it the access rate? It must be our warranty,' etc.

I do not recommend turning this into an interrogation, but what you will have achieved is a reaffirmation of the features they said they wanted in your product or service and THEY said it, so it must be true! You are then in a perfect position to hit the nail on the head and ask them the power question;

"Is it the investment required?"

At this stage you are much more likely to get a YES response. You can then follow with a sweeper;

"Apart from price, is there anything else?"

This strategy, although more complex than some, is well worth your while learning and making your own for two good reasons:

1. You are going to hear this false objection many more times and

2. When you get down to the core objection (price in most cases) you have moved the sale into a negotiation.

There is now only one obstacle between you and a happy customer; price. At this stage of the sale use the "How much too much?" question (see next tip) to begin the negotiation.

How much too much?

When a prospect says that you are too expensive, the cost is too much or your price is more than their budget allows for, this is music to a sales professional's ears. Because they know that once they have used a 'sweeper' question (is there anything else?) there is only one objection left standing between them and a successful sale.

You have to be certain that this is the genuine objection. If you get it early in the sales process, the chances are there are a number of other issues you need to cover before you can truly qualify the prospect. If this is the last objection standing then there is a real opportunity to close. We need to know the gap between our price and their 'ideal' and asking them "how much too much" is a simple and effective way to achieve this.

Once you have established the dollars, there are several strategies you can employ. By breaking down the investment over the lifetime of the product or comparing it to other products in their office, which cost more to run each day and produce less.

Remember to keep a focus on the VALUE of your offering. After you have run through and created 'value contrast' you can then use a simple and very effective trial close *(see page 5)*.

Have you met?

Some of the best and worst 'sales people' are on the street working on passers by. When I am not training salespeople, I am at my city office near the central business district.

THE WORLD'S BEST SALES TIPS

Most city centers are full of people selling charity subscriptions for various worthwhile causes. The problem is that when you have walked through this sales gauntlet several times a day, I don't get to hear very many new pitches.

I heard one recently and it was so simple and powerful I thought I would share it with you. This was a team strategy with two salesmen working the crowd. It was a busy corner and many people were hurriedly dodging and bumping into each other on their way to their office or shop.

Now as I said earlier, most people who travel around this area of the CBD are pretty immune to the efforts of street hawkers so when I overheard this technique and saw it work, I found myself a vantage spot and watched exactly how they set it up.

The first hawker standing facing the oncoming human traffic was targeting individuals in the crowd and shouting over the background noise;

> "Hi mate…have you met Paul before?"

He was using his hands to gesture first of all towards his target and then towards 'Paul'. It sounds simple, doesn't it? But as I watched, their strike rate getting passers-by to stop and talk to them was impressive.

Why did this work? Let's compare it with what all the other hawkers were doing / saying. Their typical opening pitch was along the lines of;

> "Hi there, have you got a minute to spare?"

As a closed question, it is much more likely to generate a **NO** response. I believe the first strategy worked for several reasons;

1. It was NEW to the market.
2. The prospect could not really answer with a yes or a no, because there was an initial element of doubt.
3. The chances are that most people do know someone called Paul so they stop to check.
4. Because of the tag team strategy it had a sense of an introduction rather than a cold approach.

Watching these guys operate was like observing a fly fisherman standing in a busy stream casting a line made of language and words into a packed human river and reeling them in almost instantly. I only stopped and watched for about five minutes but in that time they hooked interest almost every time.

What I think this can mean for all sales people is that our success is largely based on a balance between activity and technique. Just 'working harder' is not the solution. Finding new and creative ways of approaching our prospects and building initial interest is important.

Imagine what would happen to your sales results if you could create initial interest in only one more prospect a day, how would that translate to your bottom line?

I can't see the value

What do you say when a prospect says;

> "Thanks for coming in", or "Thanks for putting together those ideas, but we just can't see the value at this stage."

First create the impression that you are comfortable with their decision. But do not leave the conversation there. You have a great opportunity to sell here and the next time you hear a similar objection. Try this;

> "John, before I go, and for my future reference, would you mind sharing with me what sort of initiatives or ideas you see as valuable for your business?"

Then of course you shut up and scribble down all their points. If you get more than one or two, ask them which one is the #1 in terms of value over the next 12 months. Then thank them for their time and go.

You have the perfect opportunity to go over your notes in your own time and find a way to tie in your initiative to their stated values and call them back a couple of days later.

Soft shoe sales

Recently I was in a shoe store looking for a new pair of business shoes. I had spotted a pair I liked in the window of a popular shop and was 'browsing' in the shop looking and examining several different colors and designs.

As expected, a salesman came up to me and asked if I was looking for anything in particular (much better than the 'can I help you?' line). I mentioned that I would like to see the pair in the window display so he checked my correct shoe size, took me to a comfortable chair to wait and went into the back room and found a pair in my size and color.

John, the salesman, came out and in a few moments had me wearing a stylish and comfortable pair of shoes. I was walking around looking at them when I noticed that they were different to the pair I had been looking at in the window.

I mentioned this to John and he told me that as they did not have any of that size and style in stock he thought I may also like this pair just as much if not better. They also happened to be on 'special'.

What I liked about this sales pitch was that when he could not find the specified shoe, rather than give up and just tell me "sorry we are out of stock", he knew he still had a sales opportunity. He needed to get my feet into another pair of shoes! There was no hard sell and he was right, the shoes he did select are very comfortable!

Rhetoric to reality

This one is not really a tip, more a reminder. How do you turn ideas and aspirations into achievements and accolades?

As fellow sales professionals, I want to remind all of you to **WRITE** down your goals and make sure they are **TIME** based. I am sure you have heard the term; 'If you haven't got a plan, you are a tourist!' Don't be a tourist in your own life.

The power of just spending 30 minutes writing down your goals will change your life.

These have to be **YOUR** goals, not your sales manager's or your employers. If you want to enjoy the rewards, take responsibility and act NOW.

Snatching defeat from victory

Mary Pekas of the Telemarketing Institute in The United States is one of the principal architects of modern day telesales. In the late 1970's, she researched and developed prospecting systems based on that research, which are still valid and used globally today.

In conjunction with the Dartmouth Corporation and after many thousands of recorded sales calls, the Institute revealed some key metrics. These metrics are relevant to every sales person, business owner and manager who wants to improve their efficiency and effectiveness in new business sales.

Here are some of the statistics:

- 48% of salespeople give up after the first or second call.
- 20% give up after the second or third.
- 7% after the third or fourth.
- 4% after the fifth.

Quick TIP: Always bring a back up hard copy to your presentation.

It seems crazy to think that MOST salespeople give up so early in the sales process, but my experience working with many sales teams backs this up. **Almost 70% of sales people give up** either before or at three contacts / calls! Most sales managers would be delighted with such a persistent sales team but believe it or not, it is still not enough.

The key element which resonated with me when I first came across this data was that not only do almost 70% of sales people not make enough pre sales contacts with prospects but that 70% of the **PROSPECTS** they are speaking to **CAN'T** make a decision until they have had **FIVE** or more contacts with the sales person!

How many times have sales people dropped the ball or stolen defeat from the jaws of victory because they gave up after three contacts! How would making one more call or contact with your prospect change your bottom line? I don't mean call them four times in a row or indeed that the call itself will be all you have to do.

It may take three months or longer to make those four contacts and could involve e-mails, letters phone calls and or personal meetings. To do this properly you need to have a systemized way of recording the frequency of the contacts you make. I use ACT and I have also used Tracker and Goldmine. They all do a good job, but as a system, they are only as good as your input.

Once you know the disposition or dominant personality of your prospect, your prospecting becomes much easier and more effective. Earlier in the book *(see page 48)*, I discussed the four key personalities: Proactive, Protectors, Producers and Processors and how we need to treat each of them differently. The 'Pekas' research correlates with this and tells us that in the general population, approximately 15% are Proactives, 15% are Producers, 35% are Protectors and 35% are Processors. Each require a different contact strategy and sales approach.

Plan weekly - act daily

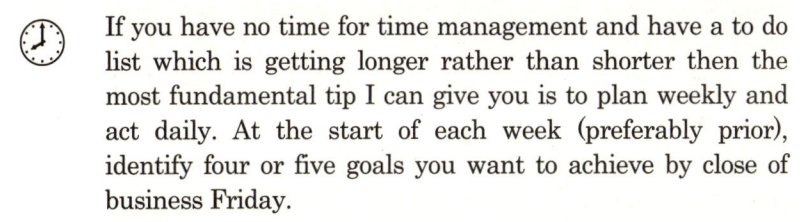

If you have no time for time management and have a to do list which is getting longer rather than shorter then the most fundamental tip I can give you is to plan weekly and act daily. At the start of each week (preferably prior), identify four or five goals you want to achieve by close of business Friday.

Identify the issues or challenges associated with each goal and then plan and diarise tasks that will negate or remove the issues. As a sales person, you need to leave at least 30 to 40% of your day unplanned.

Let's face it, unexpected events are going to happen and all a jam packed diary will do is create a sense of frustration rather than help you achieve your goals.

Readers are leaders

If I was your sales manager do you think it would be fair for me to expect that you had a keen interest in developing your own sales ability, consistently? Most sales people got into sales not by design but by accident. It was true for me and I'm guessing for you also. What I have discovered working with many sales people from many different industries is that the champions are knowledge 'sponges', they subscribe to the best newsletters, read the latest books, listen to tapes and cds and attend seminars / training events.

Most of the time the content is not new but the consistent approach means that they have confidence and choice in the techniques they use to generate business. Those who depend on their business alone to coach, train and lead them are entrusting their future development to a third party.

You may think you can't afford to buy all the great books, let me tell you why you can. Just pop down to you local opportunity or thrift shop. You can buy all the 'How to' books for about 50c each! Now you have no excuse.

In the mood

As you may know one of my founding prospecting philosophies is to make ten calls every day by 10 am! I also frequently tape my prospecting calls to listen and calibrate my performance (taping yourself is easily the best and most effective way to improve your phone prospecting performance).

A few mornings ago I arrived into work and was preparing to make my call quota. I have to admit that I was not really in the mood for making calls, handling rejection or pitching ideas over the phone. As I had been taping a few calls the previous day, I found what I thought to be a perfect excuse and decided to review yesterdays efforts.

I was surprised to find that just by listening to a few calls it got me in the mood to make some more. The first call of the day, which is often the hardest, didn't feel like the first. I recaptured the high of the previous session and was able to continue, enjoy the process and be effective.

Now I have the tape beside my phone and I can use it any time I can sense procrastination coming on. I encourage you to try it yourself.. Check your local legislation first.

From zero to hero!

Before I moved into consulting and training, I sold print advertising for about ten years. An important source of newspaper or magazine revenue is their Features list. This list of dates and features can be produced once a year or on a more frequent basis.

A features list is a list of forthcoming editorial sections that focus and specialize on a topic or area of interest to the readers, maybe fitness and dieting in a magazine for young mothers, or mobile phone technology in the business pages of a newspaper.

As a young media sales person an important strategy was to prospect to a relevant category or industry group to make them aware of this 'opportunity' and sell them into advertising in this special supplement.

Creating the prospect list was easy because the topic dictated where to focus effort. Having a sense of urgency was also simple because we had a real deadline to work towards.

For the first few months I was busy calling, mailing, faxing, emailing information on the 'feature' to supposedly interested parties only to be disappointed when it came to deadline and they never did return my calls or said "Sorry, maybe next time!"

This was one of my first sales roles, and I was one of fifteen sales reps in the company. Our weekly figures were published every Friday. After six months in the job I was still in the bottom five and I knew that my sales manager was beginning to take an 'interest' in my activities. I had to find a way to make my feature sales take off, I just needed to find the secret.

What I did helped transform my sales. I moved from almost a sales zero to a sales hero. I was consistently one of the top 3 reps in the company until I moved on. I approached the problem from a different angle that may also work for your sales performance.

When I analyzed my prospecting calls I noticed that invariably the prospect would ask me to either send them some information, or ask whether they could get any editorial in the feature. I would respond by asking them to send their information in and I would forward it to the editor's desk for review. But regularly this would end up with the 'maybe,' they would buy, IF their editorial ran. They saw this as another feature being 'SOLD' to them rather than THEIR feature, or a real opportunity they needed to act on.

What brought about the transformation in my sales was that I 'flipped' my sales approach. Rather than 'pushing' the feature to prospects I got the prospects to start 'pushing' their company's products to me.

My original pitch went along like this:

> "Thanks for taking my call Mr Prospect, the reason I wanted to speak with you today is that Power Boat Magazine are running a feature on Ski boats in next months issue and I'm calling everybody to let them know of this great opportunity"

Pretty ordinary, wouldn't you agree? So I changed to this pitch; once I had introduced myself and my magazine:

> "Mr Prospect, I'm glad I've caught you, I was speaking to my editor a few days ago and he asked me if there was much happening in the ski boat industry. I didn't know the answer, so I told him I would contact all the main companies and ask around on his behalf.
>
> So, while I've got you on the line, is there anything happening in your industry you think we should be focusing on?"

With pitch one, it sounded like a sell and he would ask me to "Send out some info". The reception was mediocre at best. But with the second pitch, they responded with excitement because of all their forthcoming new product launches, innovations etc.

After a while I thanked him for this and asked if he could send me information, and I would TRY to put it in front of the editor. In a week, my in tray was be overflowing and I had boxes around my desk from ALL the companies I had contacted.

So What! I can hear you say. Now you have to remember, I still had a ski boat feature to sell, but with my second pitch I did not mention it to the prospect and it was not the apparent basis for my call.

Here is why this tactic worked so well. A week or so later, I had received some brochures from several prospects. I then called them back with this pitch;

> "Mr Prospect, thank-you for sending the information through to me. I have shown it to my editor and he raved about it. In fact he liked it so much that he is going to put together a whole feature on Ski Boats in our next issue".

Now, it is the same feature on the same day in the same magazine, but how do you think the prospect reacted to the news of the feature? I can tell you he loved the idea, he felt he had ownership and some responsibility for it. Eight out of ten prospects approached in this way advertised and were delighted to do so and I was delighted to help them.

I know that most of you are probably not in advertising sales, but what is it about your product or service sales approach that could be reversed, changed or adjusted so that your prospect's point of view becomes one where they are selling to you or perceive that you are in a position to help them?

Crisp and Green Do - Nots

Krispy Krème Donuts are enjoying huge success here at the moment. Their marketing and market entry techniques are a lesson in good strategy and tactics. But as a lot of people are building a daily 'Doughnut' habit, I thought it worth focusing on a daily **'Do Not' habit**, particularly if you like crisp and green **CASH**. So here are a few daily 'Do Nots' for you:

- Do Not start any administrative work until you have called 10 prospects each day
- Do Not agree to internal meetings unless you know the objective and why you need to be there
- Do Not go home until you have made one last call
- Do Not check your e-mail every 10 minutes
- Do Not discuss price until you understand the value of your offer to the client
- Do Not accept the prospect's first objection as real

The 'reverse' Columbo

Earlier in the book I covered the **'Columbo'** close *(see page 87)*, based on the American detective series of the same name. One of the detective's main questioning strategies was to get the subject off guard by saying; 'before I go, there is just one thing bothering me….' The subject would relax and 'give up' a vital piece or clue.

Sales people can use this technique to great effect, but I want to focus on the occasional savvy buyer and how we can recognize when they are using a similar strategy to negotiate a better price or deal from us.

You can recognize this type of prospect in several ways;

- They have listened to your presentation and let you spend a lot of time and effort, perhaps over several meetings and discussions.
- They seem to like you more than the benefits you are offering.

- They 'flinched' when you mentioned the investment or price.

Eventually, after a pause, a phone call or popping out of the office for a few minutes, the prospect tells you they have decided that your product or service is NOT what they are looking for. This is particularly powerful in a face-to-face environment and at the end of a second or even third meeting.

They are almost apologetic. They thank you profusely for all the time, effort and work that you've put into the proposal. Telling you that maybe the next time you might win. You on the other hand feel like you have just been punched in the guts and are feeling ill about going back to the office and telling your boss that the sale that was 'in the bag!' is out!

Just as you are leaving, they say something along these lines,

> "Look John, I feel really bad about you not getting the account, just in case there is still a chance, what would be the absolute lowest price you could accept?"

Now what is the average sales person thinking? 'Yahooo! Maybe, just maybe, there is a slim chance I might be able to salvage something from this; And they drop their price. Something is better than nothing, right? WRONG! A correct response to this tactic is to defer to a higher authority. Say something like;

> "I don't know how feasible it is to do anything with the price but let me take your offer to my boss and

see what I can do for you. Just how much do you think is your limit?"

Your objective is to get a number from them that you can build value onto and increase the yield from the deal. In situations like this I prefer to leave the environment and contact them the next day with a revised offer if merited.

The 3 components of a presentation

If you are planning a sales presentation to a prospect don't just use PowerPoint and a laptop to present. Everyone does that. You will end up looking like all the rest and you will encourage your prospect to focus on price as the only way to differentiate and make a purchase decision. In every presentation you make, I recommend you divide it into three parts that you prepare for separately;

1. **The document or leave behind**
2. **The visual element (screen / ppt / whiteboard etc)**
3. **The live 'performance' or delivery**

The document should be there to SUPPORT and contain detailed notes / slides, appendices etc which do not appear in the presentation.

Do not just use a straight print out of the PowerPoint as your leave behind and don't let the prospect get hold of it before or during your presentation.

The most important part of your presentation is **your live performance** where the prospect can 'see' your passion and feel your energy. This should always be rehearsed.

A picture is worth a thousand words (and $$$)

When you are using charts in your sales presentations (I encourage you to do so) do not use too much text. You don't want your prospects reading the page, but looking at the image and its message may be different for each person in the room. You can control that message through your delivery.

Change the title of the chart. Often charts are labeled, 'sales x territory' or other equally boring titles. Change them to be more emotionally exciting, for example: 'sales x territory' could become **'+200% increase in sales!'**

Also if you are using bar charts, these lend themselves to using scaled images rather than simple boxes. Your logo for instance, could be pasted in on top of the bar chart and 'stretched' over the bar chart to make the page more exciting and visually stronger.

Images and memory

Do you find it difficult to remember numbers, particularly long ones? Generally, people find it easier to remember images than numbers. Here is an easy way to remember complex numbers. There are only 10 digits and we can combine them to make any number we want. Try this out and see if it helps. 0 = egg, 1 = pen, 2 = rubber duck, 3 = moustache, 4 = yacht, 5 = hook, 6 = whistle, 7 = nose, 8 = glasses, 9 = balloon on string.

For each number, try to associate the visual image and the shape of the number. Change the image to any other if you like. With a little practice a number like 202-456-1414 becomes a story of a **duck** laying an **egg** with a **duck** inside, this is happening on a **yacht** piloted by captain **hook** who is **whistling** a tune while using his **pen** to draw a picture of his **yacht**. The **pen** he is using is so heavy it is beginning to sink the **yacht**. Guess what? You now know the number to the White House!

Your (product) doesn't work in our business

What is your response to this type of objection? For many people in sales, their first reaction is to respond with 'interrogation' type techniques such as; How do you know? Have you ever tried our widget? What sort of system are you using now?

Where were you on the night of the murder?

Only kidding with the last one, but for the prospect it feels as if they are under investigation! Their crime, not thinking your product or service is the best thing ever invented and not welcoming your call as if you were offering them a 2 week holiday in the Bahamas! Suddenly they have to justify their beliefs and fend off hard, direct questions from someone they don't know and are probably coming to the rapid conclusion that they don't want to!

Similar objections are along these lines,

> "We used your product a while back and it didn't work", "We tried using it once and we were disappointed", or perhaps they don't buy any products in your category at all; "it's company policy not to use (product type) in our business."

What I suggest you do is this; Don't react with too many questions. Your response should be one that gets your prospect to agree with you, no matter how small the agreement. Let's look at that call again after your opening pitch:

> **Prospect**: "Your service doesn't work in our business."
>
> **Sales pro**: "Well, (slight pause and passive tone) that makes my job a lot harder, wouldn't you agree?" Pause and wait for a response.

I can just about guarantee that the vast majority of your prospects WILL agree verbally with your statement. There is a subtle, but very different, 'feel' to the communication. In the second example, your conversation is continuing from a point where **YOU BOTH AGREE** on something. In the first instance the 'interrogation' technique is founded on the philosophy of argument. I'm right and you are wrong and I'm going to prove it!

From this point you can use a variety of techniques and 'open' questions to explore and unearth the true issue / objection. Depending on the 'tone' of the conversation and the 'weight' of the decision maker I suggest that your next phrase should be about establishing whether they use ANY service like yours at the moment and if so what are their likes and dislikes.

Difficult questions

One of the BIG fears for many executives when making presentations is the dreaded Q and A session at the end, or, even worse, the interruption or unexpected question from the audience. Before your presentation begins, let your audience know whether you will accept questions during or after the presentation. If you have a large group it also helps if you ask them to stand up and introduce themselves before they ask their question. (This also reduces tire kickers).

Here is a simple five-step memory aid to help you prepare a **LEGIT** response.

- L   Listen to the whole question
- E   Echo the question back to them (repeat it)
- G   Give your response
- I   Inquire if they are happy with your response
- T   Tell an anecdote related to the question / answer

We have too much business already!

This is an unusual response to your call. You could be forgiven for thinking that it leaves you with no opportunity, but you never know. I believe it is certainly worth a couple more questions to discover the truth. The opportunity here is to get the prospect to adjust their focus from the **VOLUME** of business they are doing at the moment to the **QUALITY / YIELD** of the business.

Here is a way to respond to this type of response / objection.

"That's a nice problem to have. Before I go, most businesses I talk to have a group of key clients that they really look after, would that be true for your business as well?"

When they respond in the positive you can start focusing in on how your product or service will help them get more of those types of clients rather than just 'more' of the less profitable.

Referee

In a sales meeting your prospect may ask about previous work you have done or ask to see testimonials etc. Your sales efforts will be greatly eroded if you have to send them on at a later date or when you return to the office. If you can prepare for this event, then you will be able to close at that meeting.

Below I have outlined a response that has worked in the past for me. Pre arrange approval with two or three clients and you will increase your sales effectiveness. Let's see how this would sound:

> "John, our organization has many testimonials from some of the country's largest organizations and I will be glad to send you copies. However what I have found is that there is no substitute for first hand proof and the most effective way to do that is for you to speak to some of my clients directly. I have mentioned this to them and they are happy to take your call."

Keeping it 'LIVE' and in the moment will give you the momentum to close the deal rather than leave and greatly reduce your chances of a sale.

✓ **Quick TIP**: Let your prospect sell you – ask them what is the next step.

Checklists

The next time you have your car serviced look at the bill. Usually there will be a complete inventory of all the tasks, inspections and repairs that the garage conducted on your car. These aren't the same for every car, each car will have a different procedure dependent on the brand of the vehicle, its age and the mileage.

When your car is brought in the mechanic doesn't just look at it, pop the hood and guess what needs to be done. They have a series of diagnostic tests which are tailored for that vehicle at that moment in its life. These are essentially checklists, the right person doing the right thing, in the right order in the right way.

The most experienced mechanic will use the same system the apprentice uses. Checklists are the way to streamline and co-ordinate your sales activity so that it is more productive and profitable.

So if you find yourself or your team arriving at the office, looking at your desks and then figuring out what you should be doing you need to start putting when and what you do down on paper. These checklists don't have to be very complex. Simple and clear is the way to go.

For instance, a key philosophy of mine when running a sales campaign is 10 x 10, that is ten prospecting calls every day by 10 a.m. I also compound this by having 5 after 5, that is five sales letters after five p.m. These tasks are part of my daily activity management and I have a checklist to follow my progress.

If you don't know where to start, find the top sales person in your business and ask if you can 'shadow' them for a day or two. Observe what they do and when and write it down. You can use this as the foundation for your own series of pro forma checklists which will give you the freedom to grow your business sales.

Problem / Potential

Let's face it, if you are in sales there are going to be times when you are under pressure from deadlines, changing markets or clients backing off at the last minute. Things may vary slightly dependent on your business and your client base but the pressure to achieve becomes more about the number of sales rather than the yield of each sale.

Your buyers are not stupid, they can smell when there is 'discount fever' in the air and they are even more likely to increase the pressure on you to make a ridiculous offer.

There are two things I would like you to observe when you are in this situation,

1. Do not offer silly last minute discounts to your best, most loyal customers. This may very well provide short-term dollars, but it will come back to bite you when you are pitching at full price.

2. Use this as an opportunity to prospect and offer discounts to your competition's most loyal customers. At the very least if they do not come through, it will put pressure on them. You have to present it as YOUR problem and THEIR opportunity.

Your prospect needs to make a decision right away, before you move on to the next call. Here is an example:

After your introduction....

> "We haven't spoken before and I know your company is a big user of XYZ, I'll get straight to the point. A client of ours has just called me and has had to 'hold' off on their order until next quarter, this has left a hole in my budget and we are about to close the book.
>
> Now my problem could be your opportunity. I know the other guys are calling the market right now but I thought I would call you first and give you that chance."

The chances are very high that in the next sentence or two the prospect is going to ask you for a price. That's great, because you are now in a negotiation. When you get their best offer, tell them you have to discuss it with your manager and you will call them back in 15 minutes.

If you get three or four calls like this into the market, you will have several offers and will be in a much better position to negotiate.

Make intangible – tangible

If you sell advertising, event management or any type of service you need to find a way to make the benefit as tangible as you can. Don't just talk about all the wonderful benefits that your clients have experienced using your service, SHOW them.

If you have a client who has written you a testimonial, rather than just producing the letter, you could present before and after photos of your client. Before, with a sad, stressed expression and after, looking happy and delighted.

It may sound silly but if you can find a way to illustrate your differences and your benefits rather than simply talk about them, you will make a much stronger impression on your prospect.

Sales Letters

What is the most important part of your sales letter? It is not the letter at all, it's the envelope. When a prospect looks at their mail in the morning the first thing they will do is prioritize / differentiate between bills, letters, junk mail and those items they can't categorize.

Now I am assuming that you have the basics right, spelling, title, address etc. If your cold letter looks like it is a sales letter, guess what, it will be treated like one! My personal preference is to hand write the name and address. I find this helps cut through. When I receive hand written envelopes I tend to open them first.

Even if you have a large mail out it is quite affordable to employ a couple of 'home workers' to write out your envelopes for you.

Budget your activity

A key philosophy in my sales method is to budget my activity to my outcome. By operating this way there is a connection between what you do, how you do it and the sales result.

For many sales people seeing the 'dollar mountain' they have to climb can be a little daunting. Breaking down the dollars by quarter, month, week day or even hour is pretty straight forward but it does not necessarily help you achieve.

But breaking down your activities and then measuring on an ongoing basis allows you to quickly make adjustments to what you are doing and affect the goal.

Prioritize your prospects

Would you agree that some prospects are more valuable than others? You can easily waste time and effort on the wrong prospect. They are easy to recognize, they are usually easy to get hold of, have lots of time to see you and tend to avoid making decisions. Your activity should be prioritized according to a 'contact value' system you have set up.

Write down the six main types of roles that you prospect to and then put them in order according to their authority to make independent YES decisions (everyone can make NO decisions). This means that they have the power to decide without consulting others.

The further down the 'food chain' the less YES power they will have. Once you have them in order allocate a point value for each position. Below is my prospecting value system. Yours will be slightly different according to industry / service.

Position	Points
M Director / Owner / CEO	12
Line Manager / Head of dept	9
Senior Influencer	8
Centralized Manager:	6
Other Director	4
Company Contact	2

How this works is simple, each day I have a budgeted activity target of 20 prospecting points. Remember the old 'make 10 calls by 10am every day' mantra? Well this is a more detailed look at that system. I can reach my prospecting score by either just calling 10 firms and making ten company 'contacts' or I can maybe contact one CEO and two directors in three different firms to reach my daily target.

You can easily adapt this method to incorporate a customer relationship contact plan. Have a daily target of prospecting points and key customer contact points. Maintain your current client base AND grow new business in a planned methodical way.

Support Staff?

If you manage people, this tip is for you. Even if you don't it is still worth a look because if you are any good in sales sooner or later you are going to be given more responsibility and that usually means managing people!

One of the biggest mistakes that managers make with new members of their team is they delegate to them too soon. Of course the new employee loves this because they have a sense of control and responsibility, as do you, yet they still come to you for approval of even the smallest details.

The problems start occurring when you have a culture around you where everyone is a 'satellite' around your decision making. If you are not around the wheels fall off! When you are present you feel as if you are the only one running things. You begin to wonder what you pay all these people for!

Even the most experienced new member of your team should be managed through several stages when they first join or change their roles. That means you have to change YOUR management style.

Below I have set out my 'STAFF' model for the five management styles numbered in the order they should be deployed.

Fourth: S **Self Manage**
You can delegate to them with confidence

Third: T **They Tell You**
They are making decisions with your support and OK

Second: A **Ask and Aware**
You are constantly checking with them and are aware of their challenges

First: F **Fool Proof**
You make the system totally foolproof, checklists and task driven

Ok there were five styles and the above model only has four. What is the fifth management style? Well it is the last

F of STAFF and stands for **FIRE**! As a manager you have to be capable of firing unproductive staff. It is not a pleasant task and should not be taken lightly. But when all other avenues have been exhausted and you have made the decision, if you do not act on it, then you are not doing your job.

Stop Selling

☑ Have you ever been ready to buy a product or service but the salesman still wants to go through their presentation, even though you have said yes?

It's frustrating and many sales have been lost simply because the sales person did not recognize the buying signals and was not prepared to 'fast forward' to the end of their presentation.

My advice to you is simple, when the prospect has indicated that they WANT your product or service, **SELL** it to them. Once you have secured that sale you can then begin a whole new questioning and fact finding discussion to discover if they have any other needs. If they have, you can then either upgrade the previous sale or position the appropriate product or service.

Once your customer has made a commitment to purchase then your strategy becomes one of development, retention and service.

Questioning

There are two key reasons to question our prospects: to uncover gaps in their thinking and to uncover their meanings / interpretations.

The greatest danger is when we THINK we know what they mean, but they really are saying something completely different. This means your questioning ability is only as good as your ability to LISTEN, understand, interpret, clarify and investigate.

Listen for Generalizations

I have two favorite generalization words; 'all' and 'should'. When a prospect says something like: 'All our sales staff are excellent negotiators'. It is highly likely that the prospect is generalizing and this is a perfect opportunity to look at the prospect and say to them: 'All of them?' with a questioning inflection in the tone of voice.

When a prospect uses the word 'should' in a sentence they are usually referring to some future event, goal or outcome. It is a perfect opportunity for you to clarify their understanding.

For example, when a prospect says:

> "We **SHOULD** have our new store open by Christmas."

We can ask a **CONSEQUENCE** question;

> "Mr Prospect, what would happen if the store does not open in time?"

✓ **Quick TIP**: Discover the prospect's PAIN before you present a solution.

A word of warning here, if you instantly 'jump' every time they use a generalization and fire a question back at them, the interview will feel like an interrogation to the prospect. They will feel uncomfortable and start to 'shut down'.

Soften your questioning by relaxing you body language, keeping 'soft' eye contact, look genuinely interested in their point of view.

A simple and effective way to reduce the 'interrogation' element in your questioning and develop a more consultative approach is to 'soften' your questions with a simple phrase.

For example, when our prospect said:

> "We SHOULD have our new store open by Christmas"

Rather than responding with; "what would happen if...", Soften this by adding the phrase; "I'm curious...", or "That's interesting...", or "I'm wondering." The response then sounds like this:

> "That's interesting, (pause) I'm curious, what would happen if the new store does not open in time?"

This comes across much gentler and much more consultative in delivery. Finally, some other words which act as generalizations to listen for: Every, Always, They, Never. For example:

- "**EVERY** department is making cutbacks"
- "We have **ALWAYS** done it this way"
- "**THEY** are making some changes"

- "We have **NEVER** had to use (your product / service)"

Inquiry - interest - action

Imagine you a looking for a hotel for a short holiday for you and your young family. You are calling around gathering prices etc in order to make your final decision. What might be a typical response to this type of inquiry? You call the reception desk and after a short brief from you on what you want and a pause from the operator while they look up their price list on their booking terminal, they say something like,

> "Yes we have a suite available for those nights, would you like me to book it now?"

Nothing very persuasive in the response, just the facts and maybe a pleasant tone (if you are lucky). Now compare it to this response,

> "Oh, you're in luck, we have one suite available which would be perfect for you and your family. It is one of our largest and it has plenty of floor space. It's only two minutes from the pool and children's play area. The parent's bedroom also has its own TV and DVD player, so you can relax and enjoy your stay, would you like me to reserve it for you?"

Now, who do you think gets the business?

Why is that important?

When a prospect asks you a question, nine times out of ten you will be in a better position to help them if you respond with a clarifying question.

It is a simple technique, for instance a prospect says to you;

"Do you have that model in blue?"

You could respond with a simple yes or no and then try and close them, or you could ask a clarifying question first;

"Is it important that it is available in blue? (they respond) That's interesting, you're the third person today asking for the blue model, do you mind if ask you a question? Why it is that particular color important to you?"

If the sale was for a bowl / vase, you might discover that the prospect is planning on using it in a bathroom which is being renovated. You are then in a much stronger position to present other items which may also be of interest.

Their name is a key

What is the one word that your prospect has heard most, recognizes easiest and responds to fastest? Hey, it works on you also; it's your first name. We all love to hear it and not enough sales people use it in their selling activity.

If you are in retail sales then you most likely have a name badge. Don't let this be a reason for you not to introduce yourself. One of your first goals should be to get the name of the person you are speaking to and the easiest way to achieve this is to introduce yourself first; ...my name is John, what's yours?

When you are leaving a voice mail message try and make the first and last word you leave the prospect's name, ie: 'JOHN, it's Jim Smith here from......' and '.....I look forward to speaking to you then JOHN.'

Why don't you ask?

A client recently shared a tip with me that he has been using for years. He swears that it works like a charm every time. When I heard it I could not believe how simple and powerful it was. I have used it with great success over the past few months and I know that you are going to find it just as valuable.

Many times when you are on the phone, calling new leads and dealing with gatekeepers you are really selling the idea of an appointment before you can position your product or service. You have to get the prospect interested in meeting with you in the first place. One of the consequences of you being so keen to meet is that you can oversell. The prospect grants you a meeting simply because of the effort and the 'pleading' of your case.

These types of meetings have a habit of being postponed, cancelled or a waste of time for both parties because the prospect was never all that interested in the first place. It is a little like inviting yourself over to a stranger's house, it feels very awkward. But when you are invited over, it's easy, you're a guest, they want you to come by. Wouldn't it be great if your prospects also did the same. How easy would selling be for you if they asked YOU to come over?

The classic appointment close works along these lines,

> "...so would Tuesday or Thursday be better for you?" or "..we really should get together, how are you fixed next week?"

Both are good, but they rely on YOU selling the reason and the prospect is passive. The next time you are selling an appointment over the phone and you hear the prospect express interest in a feature / benefit of your service rather than the 'old' closes above ask them to ask you over for an appointment. Below is an illustration,

> **Prospect**: 'We are having a lot of problems with our widget fabricator at the moment.'
>
> **Sales Person**: 'Well why don't you ask me over some time next week and you can look at our new Fidget 300 system?'

It's almost invisible. But that is the beauty of this technique. When they respond, if your timing is right, their response is nearly always positive. It has become THEIR request to see you. You can also use this with follow up calls,

> "Why don't you ask me to contact your office next week to arrange an appointment?"

When you call the switchboard and get the standard "What's this in regard to?" you can legitimately say "Oh, Mr Prospect asked me to call to arrange an appointment."

Try this a few times. You will be surprised at how good it sounds and how easily it works for you and your prospects.

Review and renew

Traditional holidays are great times for businesses to review their performance. I encourage you to also review and renew your goals for the forthcoming period. Do you have written goals? If not, start today, even if they are pie in the sky aspirations they will be substantially more powerful once committed to paper.

This time of reflection also is a perfect environment to discuss what has changed in your client's world. How are they preparing for the next year? What were the successes and failures of the past year and what would they do differently if they could go back in time and change circumstances / events.

Ask them and yourself, what is the one thing which, if it could happen, (no matter how impossible it seems at this time), would change everything about your business for the better?

I can get it cheaper...

This is a familiar comment from prospective customers in a retail environment but it also presents itself when selling services and other intangible items. What is your response to this type of comment? It is critical in this scenario that we realign the prospect's understanding of PRICE. At the moment it is just a number that they are comparing with your competitors. Our job is to present VALUE in relation to price.

Here are a couple of questions you could use to design your response to this type of comment:

- Does the other company offer delivery and installation?
- Are the two product / services EXACTLY the same? What are the differences?
- Is there any sort of warranty / assurance / guarantee offered by the other company?

By investigating the details and comparing, it is usually not that difficult to differentiate two products / services which initially may have looked similar.

Morning people….

Some people describe themselves as morning people, some are evening or other 'times' of the day. Whatever you may be, identify your most productive time and then ensure that this time is dedicated to your most profitable function.

So what is your most profitable function? Draw up a list of ten core activities you are involved in each week. Prioritize them from 1 to 10 in terms of their contribution to your success. What is #1? Now take a few moments and look at an average day from dawn to dusk and ask yourself what time of the day am I most energized, passionate, and motivated?

By coordinating your diary and your biology, your work becomes a lot easier and you become a lot more effective.

There's always a niche

If I gave you one old threadbare black shoe and asked you to sell it, what would you do? What about a cheap, broken plastic pen, or a small piece of concrete, or a broken, limbless child's doll? For most of us, at first glance, these items would have no value whatsoever.

What if I then told you that that shoe was worn by John F. Kennedy when he was shot, or that the pen was the one used by Elvis to sign his marriage certificate. That the small piece of concrete was from one of the first parts of the Berlin Wall to fall and the broken doll was once owned by Marilyn Monroe! Would that make your selling job any easier?

Finding the right market can be the hardest thing to do in sales. Once you have found it the 'selling' is relatively simple. You also have to be able to PROVE that what you say is true. The fact that you say so is not good enough, an independent authority and or expert has to agree with you.

THE WORLD'S BEST SALES TIPS

"It all started when my Agent suggested I should be a bit more street smart!"

Further Reading

Bandler, Richard., et al, Reframing, Real People Press, 1979.

Berne, Eric., Games People Play, Ballantine Books, 1996.

Bettger, Frank., How I Raised Myself from Failure to Success in Selling, Fireside, 1992.

Buzan, Tony., Master Your Memory, BBC, 2003.

Caroselli, Marlene., One to One for Sales Professionals, Pearson Education, 2001.

Cialdini, Robert B., Influence: The Psychology of Persuasion, Perennial Currents, 1998.

Cohen, Herb., You can Negotiate Anything, Bantam, 1982.

Collis, Jack., Work Smarter Not Harder, Harper Collins, 1995.

Covey, Stephen., The 7 habits of Highly Effective People, Free Press, 1989.

Dawson, Roger., Secrets of Power Persuasion for Salespeople, Career Press, 2003.

Dilts, Robert., Sleight of Mouth, Meta Publications, 1999.

Essinger, James., Breakthrough Consulting, Prentice Hall, 2000.

Evans, Andrew., Secrets of Performing Confidence, A&C Black, 2003.

Fisher, Roger., et al; Getting to Yes, Penguin Books, 1991.

Flett, Neil., Pitch Doctor, Prentice Hall, 1996.

Gitomer, Jeffrey., Little Red Book of Selling, Bard Press, 2004.

Goleman, Daniel., Working with Emotional Intelligence, Bloomsbury, 1998.

Hopkins, Tom., How to Master the Art of Selling, Warner Books, 1988.

FURTHER READING

Jauncey, Phil., Managing Yourself and Others, Copy Right Publishing, 2002.

Jeffers, Susan., Feel The Fear and Do it Anyway, Ballantine Books, 1988.

Kimball, D. Scott., Top Gun Financial Sales, Dearborn, 2003.

Lampton, William., The Complete Communicator, Hillsboro Press, 1999.

Levinson, Jay., et al, Guerrilla Teleselling, John Wiley, 1998.

Maister, David H., et al, The Trusted Advisor, Simon & Schuster, 2001.

Mandino, Og., The Greatest Salesman in the World, Bantam, 1985.

Maslow, Abraham., et al, Motivation and Personality, Addison-Wesley, 1987.

Mayer, Jeffrey., If You Haven't Got the Time to Do It Right, When Will You Find the Time to Do It, Fireside, 1991

McCormack, Mark H., Success Secrets, Collins, 1990.

McCormack, Mark H., The 110% Solution, Chapmans, 1990.

McCormack, Mark H., What They Don't teach you at Harvard Business School, Collins, 1986.

Mills, Harry., Artful Persuasion, MG Press, 1999.

Morris, Desmond., The Naked Ape, Delta, 1999.

Page, Rick., Hope is Not a Strategy, McGraw Hill, 2002.

Pease, Allan., Questions are the Answers, Harper Collins, 2000.

Pekas, Mary D., Telephone Mastery: Skills for Business Productivity, Science Research Associates, 1993.

Robbins, Anthony., Unlimited Power, Simon & Schuster, 1988.

Schwartz, David J., The Magic Of Thinking Big, Prentice Hall, 1959.

Scott, Susan., Fierce Conversations, Berkley Publishing Group, 2004.

Seligman, Martin., Learned Optimism, Random House, 1990.

Ziglar, Zig., Secrets of Closing the Sale, Strand Publishing, 2003.

Ziglar, Zig., Over The Top, Thomas Nelson, 1994.

About the Author

In 2002, Ciaran McGuigan founded Early Coaching and Communication, an organization specializing in training executives in sales, presentation and communication skills.

His organization has helped some of Australia's largest and most successful companies, National Australia Bank, Macquarie Bank, Clayton Utz, Origin Energy, St George Bank, Russell Investments, Lazard Asset Management, Ricoh, News Limited and many others.

He is an Accredited Professional Speaker with the National Speakers Association of Australia and a trained practitioner in Neuro Linguistic Programming. He has a Master's Degree in Marketing from the University of Technology in Sydney and has also lectured in planning and marketing strategy at an undergraduate level.

Born in Northern Ireland, he migrated to Australia in 1991 where he now lives with his wife and two children on Sydney's Northern Beaches.

He is always happy to hear from companies and individuals from around the globe to discuss their next conference and training requirements. Please feel free to call or write.

Phone: + 61 2 9222 9112
Email: mail@earlycoach.com
Website: www.earlycoach.com